TITANIC

THE CAPTAIN SMITH INTERVIEW

CAPT. JIM CURRIE

authorHOUSE®

AuthorHouse™ UK
1663 Liberty Drive
Bloomington, IN 47403 USA
www.authorhouse.co.uk
Phone: UK TFN: 0800 0148641 (Toll Free inside the UK)
*   UK Local: (02) 0369 56322 (+44 20 3695 6322 from outside the UK)*

Published by AuthorHouse 06/21/2024

ISBN: 979-8-8230-8836-7 (sc)
ISBN: 979-8-8230-8837-4 (e)

Library of Congress Control Number: 2024912244

Print information available on the last page.

CONTENTS

Foreword

The following is a narrative based on an hypothetical meeting between a man named Edward J. Smith, and a television reporting crew. It's an attempt at providing an answer to the question: '*What if Captain Smith of the RMS Titanic had survived?*'.

For obvious reasons; the first part of this tale is entirely fictitious. However the 'meat' of the story is most certainly not, because it is based entirely on fact. It has been developed from the recorded evidence given at the two official Inquiries into the disaster.

The first Inquiry was held in America during the period -Friday, 19th of April, 1912 - which was just four days after 'Titanic' sank - and Wednesday, the 3rd of July, 1912.
The second Inquiry was held in London, England, less than a month later - between Tuesday, the 2nd of May, 1912 and Wednesday, the 3rd of July, 1912.
The reader should bear in mind that all of the evidence given under oath at these Inquiries concerned a very recent traumatic experience and it was given first hand by those who had survived that terrible tragedy. None of whom could

possibly have forgotten what occurred in the middle of the North Atlantic Ocean...the time when the brand new White Star Liner, RMS Titanic hit an iceberg and sank in just over two hours with the loss of over 1500 lives - lives which included many women and children.

Although such a loss of life at sea was not unusual when compared to the losses of life endured during the Great War, which started a little over two years later; it was, and still is to this day- the greatest ever peacetime maritime disaster.

The Captain of 'Titanic' at that time was one - Edward John Smith. He was from Bolton, England, and was in the sixty second year of his life.

Smith was also the Commodore of the White Star Line, the Shipping Company which operated 'Titanic', so was the natural choice to command their newest vessel.

Unfortunately, Captain Smith did not survive the disaster. However; using his nautical knowledge as a Steamship Master Mariner gained during a lifetime at sea, plus the aforementioned evidence blended with a modicum of imagination; the author has has resurrected the poor man and brought him into the present day to tell you his story in his own words.

In the opening scene -the TV Crew are set up in the sitting room of a quaint, Jerry-built house located in a remote forest in the extreme north of the continent of North America.

Close your eyes - imagine the scene. Now open them and read-on

PART ONE

One

SETTING THE SCENE

Good morning my friends! Welcome to my wilderness home which - being a nautical man - I have named SS 'Aidens View'. I hope you like it!

I am so glad that you managed to find your way here. Please have a seat and make yourselves comfortable. Would you like a cup of tea or coffee? No? Oh well! I'll get on with it.

However, before I start my story - let me warn you that this may take some time - perhaps several days - so if you agree; we will split it into chapters - a bit like a book. It'll mean something like a chapter or two per day.

Oh! and by the way - you can have a berth here or travel back and forth from your hotel in town each day if you wish.

Good! That's that's settled! Now, if you're ready, I won't hold you in suspense a minute longer, so let us begin...

First let me tell you that my full name is Edward John Smith and...believe it or not - I am 147 years old.

Oh! I know that's a hard pill to swallow but bear with me; all will be revealed with the passage of time - a time during which, I also hope to set the historic record straight. Actually that's why I invited you all here in the first place!

Some of you may have already heard of me, but unless you have seen the motion pictures and/or read the mountain of books and articles written about the 'Titanic' disaster, - you will not have a clue about me or what I am about to tell you. However - don't worry! you will not be alone in that respect!

I'll begin at the beginning.............

Way back at the start of the 20th Century - April 1912 to be exact - I had the honour of being the captain of the biggest ship afloat in the entire world at that time... I am of course referring to the Royal Mail Steamship 'Titanic'. Actually; except for a covered-in bit on each side of the upper deck - to the untrained eye, she did not look much different from her older sister which was the RMS Olympic. 'Olympic' was built at the same Yard as 'Titanic' which was Harland and Wolff of Belfast in the north of Ireland. and she had been in service on the England to New York run for less than a year before I took 'Titanic' on her first voyage on that same run.

At that time I was employed by a British shipping company named The White Star Line, In fact - I had been with them for most of my time as a bridge Officer. At first I served in sailing vessels and finally in steam ships.

By now, I am sure you are wondering who the heck this raving old lunatic in front of you *really* is - and where he *really* came from? However - I beg of you... have patience and all will become very clear in due course.

First let me tell you how I got here.

Many know that when I was last seen on 'Titanic', she was in her final throws, and the bridge was about to go under.

At that time; all the life-boats, except for a non- standard one had gone and there was nothing left for me to do but go back to my cabin and pick up a few personal things then put on my life jacket which was hanging on the docking telegraph.

Early, during the evacuation, I had given the ship's papers and Official Log Book to the Purser. These were contained in the ship's bag which normally resided in the Chief Purser's safe in the Purser's Office; but realising the gravity of the situation, I had called for them to be brought to the bridge, where I added the Movement Book, my Night Order Book and finally; the up-to-date Scrap Log Book.

Just before this, I had been moving around the boat deck from side with my megaphone calling instructions to those in the lifeboats which had been already launched.

The plan had been to initially fill the boats with the less able passengers such as the ladies and children, then, using the boarding ladders from the gangway doors...fill each boat to capacity with the fitter individuals from there. However, that was not to be.. I could see that the ship would not last much longer. I therefore returned the covered-in part of the bridge - set aside the megaphone and put on my life jacket. Then I turned to go through the wheelhouse to my cabin.

Just then; the ship took her final dive by the bow and at that same moment, a giant wave rushed onto the bridge and washed me and every loose bit of equipment overboard. Even more terrifying: shortly after that, the number one, foremost funnel fell over to port and nearly put an end to me there and then.

Forgive me if I do not go into detail as to the hour immediately following that experience. Suffice to say... it was a mixture of horror, hope and finally dismay.

When dawn came, I found myself part of several little islands of floating debris, but strangely enough... there were no people nearby- living or dead... just deck chairs cushions - masses of little bits of cork, a severely damaged lifeboat and last but not least - a very large barrel known as a Tun.

Up until that time, there had not been a breath of wind. The sea surface had been like a mirror and the atmosphere clear as crystal. But as sailors say..' *The wind always rises with the sun*' and sure enough - there was now a good breeze blowing and the sea was rising.

All of the foregoing caused me and my debris-companions to bob up and down in the ever-rising sea. This was useful, because reaching the crest of each wave allowed me to see what was going on at a greater distance. In addition; the sun was above the horizon and with it, the promise of yet another bright, clear spring day.

Far off in the direction of the rising sun, I could see a stationary ship with a red funnel and nearby to her; several life boats. There was also a very large area of ice just visible on the western horizon.

This was a vast ice field consisting of an unbroken line of pack ice and icebergs - some of which were isolated and others, locked in the pack ice.

I nearly burst my lungs yelling for help, but those on the ship and in the lifeboats were too far away to hear my cries. However I had a more pressing problem...the cold!

Although, for some reason - I was in an area of warmish water and wearing a uniform and heavy ridge-coat, the cold was beginning to overtake me... I had to get out of the water immediately - I could not last much longer. Then I remembered the 'Tun'.

As I said; a Tun was a very large barrel and It could hold 252 gallons of liquid, or, in this case; large amounts of salted herring.

At first I could not think of where it came from, then I remembered! There *was* such a barrel full of herring on 'Titanic's' aft well deck for the use of the steerage passengers. It must have been washed overboard during the final plunge. I made my way over to it!

Fortunately; although the lid was securely in place, it was not fastened - so I was able to remove it.

Inside, I found it quarter full of herring but there was more than enough room in there for me to join them. Additionally; the herring gave my new-found 'lifeboat' stability so it did not roll over when I clambered into it. In fact; those herring plus the supplies I found in the wrecked lifeboat and more victuals I found later on wreckage of a derelict fishing boat, proved to be my salvation.

As the sun rose, my hopes of rescue steadily receded.

Soon - another rescue ship joined the first one ...but meantime, my barrel seemed to be drifting even farther away...eastward and diagonally to the wind.

Shortly after that second vessel arrived, the one with the red funnel left but it didn't end there.

To my dismay - as soon as the first vessel disappeared from my view: the second one also left. I later learned that her captain had decided to make a circular search to the southward which was even farther away from me!

I was left alone in the middle of the ocean! Not only that, but these were the last sighting of ships I would have for a considerable time.

Two

VOYAGE TO THE UNKNOWN

As I expected - our little flotilla of barrel and debris progressed mainly eastward and northward at the will of the prevailing winds and currents.

Very soon, we were joined by part of an ancient, wrecked fishing boat.

I gathered the deck chairs and wreckage of the fishing boat in one place and made a sort of raft island with my barrel- cabin at the center. My hope was, that my 'island' would make a bigger target for potential rescuers to see or that I would somehow survive and eventually arrive on the shores of Ireland, Scotland or even the Azores.

It was Spring and it was getting warmer each day. The weather remained clement and continuously improved as the days and weeks went by.

I survived on herring and biscuits and water which I had salvaged from the tanks of the damaged lifeboat boat. This, I supplemented with rain water.

Eventually; I realised that I was heading North and even a little West. It occurred to me that my little 'island' of hope was being carried in the reverse direction in which the ice bergs were carried south by the Labrador Current.

One bright morning when I awakened; I saw before me a massive Ice cliff in the distance. The sun was rising behind me so I knew we were heading westward.

This cliff stretched north to south as far as the eye could see. Even worse; my craft was under the influence of a local current which was taking me toward it.

As we got nearer, I could see that I was being rapidly taken directly toward a crevice in the cliff.

Soon I passed through a narrow portal in the cliff-face and to my amazement, fount myself in a vast ice cathedral floored with an incandescent green pool of flat calm water.

At the top end of this 'cathedral' lay an ancient, perfectly preserved wooden sailing ship which reminded me of paintings I had seen of Sebastian Cabot the Arctic explorer.

In the forlorn hope of finding living souls, I shouted, but all that came back to me was my own voice following its echoes all around me.

Three

TEMPORARY
ACCOMMODATION

Eventually, my little flotilla came to rest against the side of the abandoned ship. I climbed out of my refuge and promptly fell over... I had forgotten how to walk!

However, after much effort I eventually began to explore my new home.

It was amazing! Everything was as if the previous crew had just gone ashore

There was even oil in the oil lamps and flour in the flour barrels.

Very quickly I found flints and managed to get a fire going and light an oil lamp.

There was no evidence whatsoever as to who the previous occupants had been but it was obvious that they had left many years previously. However, they did not leave by boat because the lifeboats were still stowed in their davits. So where did they go? I might never find out, but by the style of the abandoned ship; it was most certainly a very long time previously.

I settled-in to my new surroundings and very quickly- despite my age- the invigorating atmosphere of the place returned me to full health and fitness. In fact I felt as though the years were being shed from me like an old skin.

After several weeks, I settled-in, but I was falling asleep for increasingly lengthy periods and I had no way of knowing the time. date or even the year.

Then one morning when I awoke after what seemed like an endless sleep - I found that my world had changed. It was then and by sheer accident that I discovered where the previous occupants did go.. or at least - the direction they took when they left.

During my 'beauty sleep', a partial melt of the 'Cathedral' walls had taken place. This revealed a passage leading farther into the cliff.

I decided to explore this passage; expecting it to be endless or to lead to another cavern. To my amazement - after only about an hour of walking, it suddenly opened out into a vast dense forest of towering pine trees, the floor of which, was carpeted by gray fern-like plants. There were no animal or bird sounds and nothing moved. The atmosphere was still and pleasantly warm....Sheer paradise!

When next we meet, I will tell you how it finally happened that I am now sitting in front of you.

After that... I will tell you what I have discovered as to what you and the world think happened on 'Titanic' but more important - what really happened that fateful day.

Four

SETTING-UP HOME

Good Morning! Welcome back aboard Nice to see you again. Sit and have a cup of tea and I will continue.

Last time, I told you how I survived the 'Titanic' disaster and how I got here. Now, I will carry on and tell you what transpired immediately after I arrived back on dry land.

You may well imagine that my first thought after finding the old sailing ship locked in the ice, would have been to try returning to civilization using one of her lifeboats and you'd be correct. However - the discovery of my forest paradise changed my mind. I decided to set up a new home in the forest. Then when settled there - I would explore farther.

Eventually and before the onset of autumn, I had removed much of the essentials from the old ship to a clearing I found in the forest. There, usings parts of the old ship, I constructed a substantial habitat and settled down before winter arrived.

I had found weapons flint and powder in the old ship as well as a hoard of lead.

I also discovered that I was not alone... there were deer and small mammals in the forest, consequently, I was able to supplement my diet with fresh meat. However, I also discovered that the strange gray fern was also pleasantly edible. and have since deduced it to be the reason for my longevity.

And so....The years passed without sight or sound of another human...but loneliness did not concern me. After all a ship's Captain is the loneliest man on his ship so I was used to it.

However, as time passed, I noted that I did not seem to be getting much older and I was getting a little bored with my own company. Therefore; one day, I made up my mind to go and search for others. As I said - I had no way of telling time or date but I was soon to get an enormous shock.

I started in Spring and headed southward - carefully marking my trail to ensure I could find my way back home.

After a while, I began to hear strange sounds in the sky, then to my amazement - I saw this enormous silver flying machine roaring its way over my head and it seemed to be getting lower as it did so. ....I was terrified! My mind was in a turmoil! Had I been transported to an alien place?... Were there really people on other planets? and was I now on one? You can only imagine what thoughts were frantically chasing each other across my poor, confused old brain at that moment.

I did not stop but kept walking. Suddenly! I tripped

and fell down an embankment between two giant trees and landed on the hard surface of a deserted road.

My heart was still beating like an ungoverned steam engine when to my horror... a very strange stream-lined vehicle - on the ground this time - passed me at a speed I had never seen any vehicle move. Suddenly it stopped and came screeching backward toward me.. I was about to run back to the safety of the forest when this perfectly normal voice with an American accent asked me if I was OK and would I like a 'lift'?

I had no idea what the man was talking about (You must remember that the last 'lift' I saw was on the sinking 'Titanic' and it lifted people between decks and was manned by a 'Lift Attendant'.) However the man explained what he meant. He seemed pleasantly normal, So I accepted his 'lift'.

From the moment I entered the vehicle, I decided not to relate my history to him or for that matter - anyone, until I found out what kind of world I had arrived in. Fortunately my 'good Samaritan' was extremely talkative so I had little to say.

He told me that he was a member of a Club called 'Naito' or something, and that he lived in a new town nearby. I pretended to understand until at one point he referred to 'the turn of the century'. Now that really puzzled me.

I had left my world at the beginning of the 20th Century so what 'century' was he referring to?

I did not wish to appear stupid to this kind man, but how to go about it without doing so? Then I had an idea!

I asked him if he had heard about the 'Titanic', knowing that such a disaster would be world news.

I nearly fainted when he replied:

"Funny you should say ask sir. The new movie is coming to our local movie theater soon." He went on-
"Gosh! just think that terrible disaster happened eighty five years ago." Adding: *"I wonder if there are any survivors still alive?"*

It hit me like a ton of bricks! I must have gone into a Methuselah-like sleep way back when I first arrived here and I had been transported to the year 1997. I also wondered what the hell a *movie* was!

In a very short space of time, we arrived at a substantial town - and from that moment my brain was filled with strange new sights, sounds and wonders. However; to my joy and relief; I found that I was still on Mother Earth. Thereafter, the development of science and technology kept me awake for months on end.

Very quickly - I managed to obtain work in the town but decided to keep my past and my forest dwelling a secret... which - by the way - it still is to this day. No one asked questions so I did not offer any explanations. Consequently; I would be obliged if you keep this location a secret.

That first working week, I earned some money and found out what a *movie* and a *movie theater* were and where these wonders were located. I also found out when this movie about 'Titanic' was to arrive in town - I had a little time to wait.

Eventually, in the spring of 1998, the moving picture 'Titanic' arrived in town. By then, the wonders of moving pictures were no longer a 'wonder' to me and I settled in my movie-house seat to witness what was billed as the story of the 'Titanic' disaster.

I was astounded by the accuracy with which my ship had been re-created. However, any resemblance between how the voyage and eventual disaster was depicted was vaguely coincidental. I won't go into detail at this moment. Later, I will compile a list of inaccuracies I saw at that time and have learned subsequently from research into official documents.

I fell into a regular routine. /During the week, I stayed in lodgings in town, but returned here to the old 'SS Aidens Brae' each weekend.

Over the passing years, I carried out improvements until the place ended-up as you see it today.

Since that day at the movie theater, I've been catching-up with the events in history which I missed. As I said; I have seen the movie 'Titanic' and other such accounts and have read the evidence given by the survivors of the disaster. I have even become computer-literate and am now fully aware of the opinions of the wider world.

I was, and still am, amazed by the wonders of the world around me. However; as I learned more, I gradually became more and more annoyed with the public perceptions concerning the 'Titanic' disaster itself. It was then that I decided to contact you and offer to tell you the true story of what really happened leading up to the death of 'Titanic' and all those poor souls who perished with her.

Ah! I hear 8 bells! That sound tells me that lunch is on the table. Please join me; we can continue in the afternoon.

Five

APRIL 10 1912

Well! now that the inner self has been satisfied - we will - if its all right by you - cut the preliminaries and get back to my story.

First - allow me to start at the proper place... the beginning!

To do this, I take you back to quarter past the hour of Noon on Friday the tenth of April in The Year of our Lord, 1912. That was the final moment when 'Titanic' had any connection to dry land - the moment she set sail on her maiden voyage to the City of New York in the Americas.

It was a beautiful spring day when we left Southampton. The sun was splitting the heavens and there was barely a breeze to ruffle the beards of the onlookers. It was so sunny and mild that some of the female well-wishers on the quay-side were dressed in hats and dresses the likes of which would not have been out of place in mid-summer. In fact; I remember seeing one very elegant lady decked out in a full brimmed floral hat and a long, white summer gown walking briskly along the quay-side as we moved out of our berth.

There was but one mis-hap and that was just after we had cleared the White Star Dock and starting the long journey down river toward the sea. It was caused by 'Titanic' displacing water near to moored ships as we passed them. One of these was the SS New York. As we were passing her, the water displaced by our hull, caused her to part her stern lines and drift out from her berth toward us. Fortunately; our local Pilot acted quickly and the attending tugs were able to limit the problem. Consequently; we were delayed for little more than thirty minutes and apart from a broken mooring line or two on the other ship - there was no damage.

On our voyage to New York, we stopped twice briefly to embarque passengers. Our first stop was at Cherbourge in France that same evening of the day we left Southampton.

We anchored in Cherbourge's outer harbour but I can't remember if any passengers left us there, however we did embarque a few. This was done using a small ferry-like vessel.

Our next port of call was at Queenstown in southern Ireland. That was the next day - on April 11th. At that time Ireland was part of the British Empire. I have since learned that it is now a separate country and they have changed the name of Queenstown to 'Cove'.

At 11 am local time on April that day, we anchored outside the port of Queenstown. Thereafter; another ferry-like small vessel brought more passengers for New York and a few left us there.

At 1.30 pm that afternoon of April 11, we weighed anchor and thirty minutes later - at 2 pm; we passed the well-known Irish land mark of Daunt Rock and I ordered the engines Full Away on Passage. They would remain so until that fateful morning of April 14.

I have crossed and re-crossed the North Atlantic ocean more times than the shuttle crosses a weaver's loom, yet never, up until that April weekend, did I see a more benevolent face to that body of water. In fact, I remember remarking to my Chief Officer Wilde that it was just as well that 'Titanic' was not a sailing ship; otherwise we would have become becalmed off the. Irish coast all weekend. Poor lad! Since then I have learned that he was lost in the disaster. What a waste! He was at the height of his career and marked for command.

Anyway - the voyage started off perfectly. We had the very latest wireless machines and two operators supplied by Marconi...you know - the lad who invented the thing.

These lads were at their instrument 24 hours of the day -every day of the week. Most of the messages they sent or received were by or for the passengers. However, some were for my attention.

In fact; The Marconi Company had laid down a protocol concerning the level of importance to be given to messages by type. Navigation warnings which might effect ship priority took precedence. These included ice-specific warnings. Next were messages specifically addressed the the captain. All other messages of a general nature - including passenger messages - were classed as non- urgent.

During the first two days out from Queenstown, I received messages of good luck from other captains on the North Atlantic run. Two of these I remember in particular. The first was from the Cunarder RMS Caronia and the other, from one of our own ships.. the RMS Celtic.

Now this is where we start to put things right!

Since I have been back in touch with the world I see that among a multitude of stories about my actions - It is stated that I received Ice Warnings from these two ships. I must tell you here and now -.that is utter balderdash! I received nothing of the kind.

Contrary to what lands-folk think; an Ice warning is specific, it does not contain - as these ones did - things like good wishes and general gossipy remarks. In fact the one I got from the 'Coronia' was received two days before the disaster... just after morning sights on April 12. It simply included second hand information regarding ice - ice that was situated way to the north of where 'Titanic' would eventually pass. I remember showing it to Lightoller my Second Officer and his Navigator, Boxhall.

The 'Celtic' message was received in the early afternoon of April 14 and was couched in the same terms as the one from 'Caronia'. It too included second hand information concerning ice. This time, the ice in question was 10 miles to the north of where 'Titanic' would eventually pass and in the same general region as the ice mentioned in the 'Caronia' message.

Now my friends! I know these waters like the back of my hand, and this includes the fact that ice in that part of the ocean in early spring, moves north and eastward...in fact it moved continuously further away from where 'Titanic' was going to be.

Goodness me!..'Titanic' and all other west-bound vessels were following an agreed track designed by an American chappy named Maury. Ironically: he designed it to take ships safely south of the then know iceberg regions during the Spring and Summer months. The same precautions prevail to this day!

Heavens! I distinctly remember, that after I received that message from the 'Celtic' I showed it to the Navigator on duty and he plotted it on the chart. After that, I put it back in my pocket and went for a walk.

During my walk, I met young Ismay our Chairman and since it came from one of our own Company ships, I gave it to him to read.

Ismay had decided to join us on that maiden voyage, and at the time I met him - he was chatting to a couple of rather charming ladies.

On looking at the message, he expressed concern, about the word 'ice', but I assured him it was of no consequence. In fact, I told him to keep the message and I'd get it back from him later.

However, that was not the only message containing the word 'Ice' that I received.

Later that afternoon, I was on the bridge to witness the 6 pm. change of Watches. As I talked with 2nd Officer Lightoller, our wireless man handed me a copy of a proper ice warning he had overheard and later received from the Leyland Line ship 'Californian'. Her operator had offered it to him as a matter of courtesy. It simply confirmed the positions of icebergs in the same vicinity as the ones mention in the much earlier 'Caronia' and 'Celtic' messages.

Now that 'Californian' message was indeed a proper ice warning and as I had suspected...showed that the ice was moving eastward along the latitude line of 42 degrees North... nothing to concern us at all but of great importance to ships traveling to and from areas of the North American seaboard north of New York.

These vessels normally employed a method of navigation called 'Parallel Sailing'. This meant they sailed along a parallel of latitude...in this case; the latitude of 42 degrees North-the very line along which lay the ice!

However, I should point out to you - I did not completely ignore any of these mentions of ice, and despite popular opinion...and my then, advanced age of 62 years, I was not a confused, mentally diminished old fool.

From experience, I deduced that the ice mentioned in the 'Coronia' message had been carried across our intended westward path by the Gulf Stream. I also knew that although deep draft ice such as bergs moved more readily with the current - lighter stuff often lagged behind. Consequently, after dinner that evening I gave instructions in my Night Order Book for all bridge Watch-keepers and Lookouts to be alert for the possibility of meeting with light ice'. Such ice would not sink us but could cause damage.

Additionally; all Watch Officers were specifically ordered to call me if in the least bit of doubt, including a reduction in visibility.

Well gentlemen! This is as far as I'm prepared to go concerning ice at this time.

At our next session - I will first take you back to just before Noon on Sunday, April 14 and thereafter - step by step - to each event throughout that afternoon and evening - right up until the sound of 'Titanic's' engine telegraph brought me rushing onto my bridge and until I lost my ship to a little, rogue ice berg.

It's time for my afternoon tea and suspect you will be anxious to get back to your hotel. We will get together again tomorrow.

Thank you for your patience. I'll see you all again tomorrow morning.

Good Afternoon!

$\mathcal{S}ix$

NOON SIGHTS

Hello! and and a good morning to you all once again. I trust you have been well and had a relaxing evening.

At the end of our last conversation - I said I would take you back to just before Noon that Sunday of April 14, so here we go again!

On all British ships, it was customary that on a Sunday morning at sea, off-duty crew would be mustered on the boat deck for what was known to sailors as 'Board of Trade Sports'. Officially it was called Board of Trade Boat and Fire Drill and it was for crew members only - passengers were not involved!

At that time, Deck Crew would muster at their allotted boat stations on the boat deck. The boat equipment and contents would be checked but no boats deployed. Fire hoses and other fire-fighting equipment would be deployed and the hoses tested.

However, that morning -although the sky was clear - there was an icy-cold brisk wind blowing from the north...

blowing against our starboard side. Only the port side decks were sheltered enough to warrant having crowds of unsuitably clothed men standing around doing nothing. Consequently; since the crew had been fully tested at Fire and Boat Stations in port no more than three days previously and most were seasoned sailors, I decided to postpone that drill.

As on all British merchant ships; just before twelve o' clock, the senior bridge Officers and Captain assembled on the bridge for what was known as 'Noon Sights'. 'Titanic' was no different!

This was to determine the true position (latitude and longitude) of the ship at that moment and the exact local time.

It involved the use of an instrument called a sextant to measure the altitude of the Sun above the horizon at the moment it was due South or North of the ship...You will know this as 12 o' clock Noon. The same principal applies in every part of the world...not just at sea.

Anyway! That morning - myself and Wilde together with First Officer Murdoch and Second Officer Lightoller, assembled on the port bridge wing and at a given moment - using our sextants - we measured the altitude of the sun above the horizon. The chronometer time of this event was noted by the junior Navigation Officers in the Chart Room. Thereafter - the calculation was made and the ship's position established. Also - at that same time - any minor error in the ship's clock time relative to the time on the chronometer was found and adjustments made accordingly. Many folk, including modern navigators, think that the adjustment of the ship clock at that time to match the chronometer was connected to daily routine. They are only partly right.

Navigation back then was, as I say, by sextant observation which required accurate Greenwich Mean Time. However; only one ship's clock kept accurate GMT and that was the Chronometer. It follows that if the chronometer suddenly broke down, the Navigators would be in deep trouble. Therefore; the ship's clock time was always adjusted to be accurate relative to the chronometer so that if the latter broke down, the Navigators could be reasonably confident with results obtained using the time showing on the ship's clock.

The results that Noon of April 14, 1912, showed that 'Titanic' was not where she should have been. She was not on her intended track; but a little to the south and eastward of it. Obviously the northerly wind acting on the starboard (right) side and on our four giant sail-like funnels, had pushed her (sailing ship -like) off track! Consequently, when the results of the Noon sights were known; the course was adjusted to the right to compensate and ensure that we would arrive exactly at our intended turning point.

This turning point was an unmarked position in the ocean known to Western Ocean men as 'The Corner'. (For the Technically minded it was Latitude 42º North-Longitude 47º West.)

At that time we were nearing the end of a long, curved track from Ireland. Since I knew the total length of that track and how far 'Titanic' had traveled along it at that moment; then by simple arithmetic, I deduced that from Noon that day, we had about 126 miles to run before turning 'The Corner'. My next task was to determine the time we should arrive there and turn the ship. To do this

I needed an estimate of the speed we would make during that afternoon.

The Noon Sights had also shown me that my ship had averaged a little over 22 knots between Noon the previous day - April 13 - and Noon that day of April 14. This was very encouraging. However, I knew that unless I increased engine speed; 'Titanic' would not keep-up that average speed. Because I also knew from long experience, that in that area, we would encounter a head current which would slow us down long before reaching the turning point'...so I erred on the safe side and allowed a speed of 21.5 knots for the rest of the Afternoon. Since we had about 126 miles still to run from Noon before turning, that meant that we would arrive at 'The Corner' at 5-50pm in the late afternoon.

Throughout the rest of the day, we had fine weather - the skies were clearing and the barometer was rising. This, in turn, told me that the wind would soon drop, and that we were entering an area of high barometric pressure; commonly known as a 'High'.

I also knew from experience that when we turned 'The Corner' the influence of any current holding us back, would diminish or even disappear and we would increase speed without increasing engine revolutions.

Then I had to consider the question of time on the ship's clocks. We were heading westward; this meant that as well as the clocks being accurate at Noon each day; we would need to retard the ship time every midnight if we wanted the ship's time to agree with New York time when we arrived there.

Up until Noon 14th, we had been retarding ship's clocks 44 minutes each night. However, after turning at 'The Corner' we would be heading more directly westward so would need to retard them a little more each night. This turned out to be 47 minutes.

By tradition, clock changes were split evenly between the 8 pm to Midnight Watch and Midnight to 4 am Watch. The first one was the junior Watch so in this case, since it was an uneven number of minutes to be changed; that Watch would attract the lion's share of 24 minutes.

At 5-45 pm. I went onto the bridge. It was the first 'dog Watch' and my First Officer Murdoch was in charge.

As the ship time approached 5-50 pm. everyone was standing-by. The junior navigation officer standing ready beside the chronometer in the chart room.

When the hands on the chronometer read 8-48 GMT, (the equivalent of 5-50pm on the ship clock) the junior yelled 'time' and I gave the order "Bring her round to North 71 and a half West". This was repeated in turn by the Junior Officer beside the Quartermaster (helmsman) and he - in turn- repeated it as he applied the helm.

In a few moments came the confirmation from the helmsman ... "North 71 and a half west she is Sir". I responded with "Steady as she goes Quartermaster."

At that moment - if 'Titanic' had turned as I had planned (and hoped) - exactly at the position of 'The Corner', she would then be on her final approach toward her destination - New York...but did she and was she?

Seven

EARLY EVENING

After the ship had settled onto her new track, I remained on the bridge to witness the change of Watches which was due to take place at 6 pm. At that time, my Chief Officer Wilde would hand over charge of the bridge to my Second Officer Lightoller. At the same time; the Junior Navigating officers would also change. Then, my Third Officer Pitman and 5th Officer Lowe would take over in the Chart Room. At the same time, the Patent Log reading would be relayed from the stern by the duty Quartermaster using our telephone system and the result would be recorded in the Scrap Log Book.

At 6 pm, four bells were sounded and shortly after that, the phone rang in the wheelhouse. It was the Patent Log reading report!

The Log reading proved my worse fears - the 'Titanic' had indeed been slowed down by an ocean current which had been pushing her backward. In fact: instead of her slowing to 21.5 knots as I had planned for - the reading at 6 pm showed that she had been slowed even more - to a little under 21.0 knots. - 20.95 knots to be exact.

Not only that: but earlier-on in the afternoon, our giant funnels would have been, as I said earlier: acting like the sails of a sailing ship and the northerly wind blowing against them would also have pushed the ship southward. In short: 'Titanic' was not where I wanted her to be, which was right on the straight track that would bring her to her destination.

I suspected that she had turned a few miles to the eastward of 'The Corner'. However; the weather was fine and clear and the clouds were rapidly dispersing. This meant that at dusk, Lightoller would be able to take observations by sextant of the stars and planets and find out where we really were. Then, if necessary, we would be able to adjust our course and bring 'Titanic' back onto her intended track.

I remained on the bridge for a few minutes after Lightoller had taken charge. After that, I left the bridge and went to my cabin to change for dinner.

That evening; instead of entertaining selected guests at my table in the First Class Dining Room; I was to be the guest of honour at the table of prominent first class passengers in the Cafe Parisienne.

The Watches would change again at 8 pm so, as was my normal practice; before dinner I would visit the bridge and at that time, fill in my Night Order Book and have a chat with the Officer of the Watch.

Eight

EIGHT PM

Shortly before 8 pm, I made my way to the bridge and filled- in my Night Order Book. When 8 bells sounded I heard the lookouts acknowledging them then I joined Second Officer Lightholler out on the bridge wing.

It was now almost completely dark but by the flat calm state of the sea, it was obvious that the wind had completely gone. However; the slap- bang of our breaking bow waves - the strong ship-generated breeze blowing in my face from right ahead, and the now obvious vibration, told me that 'Titanic' was picking up speed.

I told Lightoller that I had filled in the Night Order Book, so he left briefly and went indoors to the Chart Room. Having read and signed it he returned to his post beside me on the bridge wing. He would remain there until relieved by First Officer Murdoch at 10 pm.

During our short conversation, Lightoller told me that he had obtained six very good sextant observations just after 7-30 pm that evening. Three of these were to determine Latitude and the other three to find our Longitude and that even as we spoke, the Junior Officers were hard at work in the Chart Room making the long, laborious calculations which would tell me exactly where 'Titanic' was at the time the sextant observations were taken.

Among other things, we discussed the earlier messages mentioning ice.

Although we both knew that the danger was well to the north of our intended track; we agreed that their might be the odd light ice trailing behind. We also agreed that if the flat calm conditions prevailed - we would have a hard time detecting it. Consequently; Lightoller ordered the Lookouts in the Crows Nest to keep a sharp lookout for small ice and to have the order passed-on to their reliefs.

We estimated that we would be in the longitude of the ice reported by the SS Californian in about an hour's time, at around 9 pm and at the farthest west reported longitude at around 11 pm.

With these few words, I left Lightoller and retired to enjoy my dinner. As I passed through the Chart Room, I remember seeing young Boxhall studiously bent over his work book, calculating the celestial observation taken by Lightoller earlier. He told me that he would have them completed for me before 10 pm. That suited me fine, since I would be visiting the bridge at 10 pm to witness Lightoller's hand-over of the Watch to my First Officer Murdoch.

Nine

TEN PM UNTIL?

After a very pleasant dinner, I returned to my Day-room and settled down to write a letter home. I would post it when we arrived at New York. I remember thinking - *Heavens! there's a very good chance that if we get a scheduled turn-around at New York- we will be back in England before this letter finally arrives at it's destination.*

Shortly after 9-30 pm. I finished writing - put my bridge coat on and headed for the bridge.

Before I reached the curtained doorway to the main chart room, there was the sound of a knock and the curtain was pulled aside at the same time.

Young Boxhall had arrived with the position calculated from Lightoller's sextant observations. He gave them to me, and as he stood by the door; I plotted the position on my own chart which was spread-out on my chart desk. Strangely enough, I remember it clearly. It was Latitude: forty degrees fifty four minutes North - Longitude: forty seven degrees, forty five minutes West and it confirmed that until that time; we had not attained the previous day's average speed of 22.1 knots. It also confirmed that 'Titanic was a little south of her intended track. I remember remarking; "she made 21 up until 6 pm - she's most certainly making more than 21 knots now".

I left Boxhall back in the main Chart Room and made my way out onto the pitch dark bridge wing where I arrived beside Lightoller and Murdoch. The former was in the act of handing - over the Watch so I stood back until the formalities had been completed. After Lightoller had left, I had a brief conversation with Murdoch.

Murdoch was not what you might call a 'dour Scot'; in fact he was a brisk, lively individual who was destined for a successful career at sea. I had every confidence in him - he was the sort of man that any captain wanted beside him in a tight situation. Little did I know then, that it would not be long before the poor lad proved his worth!

About 10-15 pm, I left the bridge and headed back to my day room. My steward brought me a cup of tea then I stretched-out, fully clothed, on my settee with a good book. I intended to follow my usual practice of witnessing the clock change at midnight.

As I said - the usual practice was to divide any planned clock change between the 8pm to Midnight duty Watch and the following Midnight to 4 am duty Watch. In this case it would be 24 minutes the first time and 23 minutes thereafter to complete the total planned change.

The first amount would be applied when the bridge clock first read 12 Midnight. At that time, 'Titanic' would have been on the final course for New York a total of 6 hours and 10 minutes from when she turned at 5-50 pm and a total of 12 hours when they had been last set at Noon. Also, at that time automatic clocks would be stopped and the bridge clock would be set back to read 11-36 pm. However 8 bells would not be sounded because that was not the end of the Watch on duty - they had another 24 minutes of work to complete.

When the clock once again read 11-45 pm, One (1) bell would be sounded - not as a clock time, but to warn all those who were awake that 15 minutes remained before the duty Watches would change.

Normally at that time- if all went to plan -, the Stand-by Quartermaster would awaken the next duty Watch consisting of 3 Quartermasters, Third Officer Pitman and Sixth Officer Moody. The latter two would take over from Fourth Officer Boxhall and Fifth Officer Lowe.

Again; under normal circumstances - when the clock once again read 12 midnight, 8 bells would be sounded and the duty Watches would change. At that time, Pitman would take over and would complete the planned change by setting the clocks back an additional 23 mins. turning the ship's bridge clocks back to 11-47 pm.

When these clocks read 12 o' clock midnight for the third time, the slave clocks would be re-started and that would put all ships clocks on April 15 time. Incidentally - the senior officers did not keep the same duty Watch times as the aforementioned junior officers. They changed over at 10 pm - 2 hours before the clock read 12 0' clock midnight for the first time. Like me; they spent the entire of extra minutes clock change in bed. As they say; 'Rank hath privilege!'.

Some of the passengers waited up to adjust their watches at that time. Others waited until they were called the following morning. Whereas; most of the day-working crew would be asleep and would have set back their watches and clocks by the full planned amount before retiring.

Since these clock changes were made using the chronometer (the most accurate time piece on any ship) as the reference point- I and many others waited until the slave clocks were reset and started at the new ship time before adjusting personal time-pieces.

Ten

WHAT WAS THAT?

I was stretched-out and half asleep on my settee. The book I had been reading had fallen over my face - jerking me almost fully awake. However; a second later, there was a sort of 'sensation'. I can't in all honesty say that I actually felt anything. However there was nothing wrong with my hearing. The shrill, unmistakable *trilling* of the engine telegraph bells on the bridge had me up and grabbing for my Bridge-coat. At the same time, I looked at my Watch and it was reading about a minute after Midnight. In a second, I was on my feet; shrugging-on the heavy coat and simultaneously opening the door to the main chart room. It was then that I felt the ship 'shuddering'.

The chart room was deserted so I made my way through the curtained doorway into the wheelhouse where I found the Sixth Officer standing behind the Quartermaster at the helm. I noted that the telemotor tell-tale was indicating that the helm was hard over to starboard - meaning that the QM had been given a hard-left turn order and that the compass needle was swinging toward the WSW. I did not stop, but continued at a rate of knots out into the covered area of the bridge.

At first - coming from a lit area - I had difficulty making out who was there - if anyone, but I wasn't struck-dumb. I raised my voice and asked the darkness - "What was that? What did we hit".

The reply brought me to an abrupt halt.. I was gaining my night vision and by it, made out the shadowy figure of First Officer Murdoch. He was standing in front of the compass binnacle - almost amidships.

"It was an iceberg, sir! I tried to go to port around it but it was too close and we hit it with the starboard bow."

Immediately I ordered him to close the watertight doors in the main watertight bulkheads, using the automatic lever mounted on the bulkhead under the center window - and to ring the alarm bells.

Murdoch assured me that he had already done so. He also told me that he had ordered the engines to Full Astern to bring the ship to a halt.

I had noted this on the 'tell-tale' arrow of the telegraph and the ever-increasing vibration caused by propeller cavitation confirmed this to be so.

As we were talking - 4th Officer Boxhall was standing behind us, and the standby Quartermaster had just returned from an errand. I immediately ordered the Quartermaster to go and find the Ship's Carpenter and have him find out if we were making water in any of the compartments deep in the bowels of the ship. I then turned to send Boxhall below to look for damage, but found that he was already on his way to have a look.

I went over to the port wing of the bridge and looked toward the stern. Very soon I could see the white circle of foam from the wash of the churning propellers spreading out around it like a slowly opening flower. This told me that 'Titanic' was almost stopped dead in the water, so I grabbed hold of the telegraph handles and stopped the engines.

A mere three minutes had passed from hitting the ice and by then, 'Titanic' was pointing in a south-westerly direction. At that same moment, the standby Quartermaster returned to the bridge and told me that he had found the Carpenter and that the man was already carrying-out his duty.

At that time; I did not think there was a serious problem. 'Titanic' had come to complete halt so, when we were stopped in the water - in anticipation of resuming the voyage - I ordered the engines ahead and at the same time; ordered the Quartermaster at the helm to turn her hard a port (hard right) and bring the bow of 'Titanic' back to the direction in which she had been heading before the incident happened. I needed a burst of power and a hard-over helm because a rudder does not work on a stopped ship.

While all this was happening and as a precaution - in case there was any more ice in the direction of the turn; I stood watch looking ahead on the port side of the bridge while Murdoch did the same on the other. side.

Very quickly, 'Titanic' was heading on her original course and I brought her to a standstill once more. Thereafter; I joined Murdoch on the starboard bridge-wing and looked to see if we could see the iceberg culprit. At that same moment, Boxhall returned from an inspection tour and reported that

41

he had not found any damage - just a powdering of ice on the forward well deck. Thereafter, by straining our eyes, we could just make out the low-lying shape of the iceberg a little astern and to the left. Boxhall had a problem seeing it since he had just emerged from the lit interior of the ship and his night vision had not been fully restored. After that, I went into the wheelhouse and had a look at the angle-of-heel indicator.

All seemed normal, so I sent Boxhall to find the Carpenter and tell him to *hurry-up!*.

At the same time, I sent the standby Quartermaster with a note to the Chief Engineer to ask him to do something about the deafening noise caused by the venting steam exiting from the boilers via the vent in funnel number one right above our heads. It was impossible to issue orders or hear anyone speak due to the ear-splitting roar it was making.

As with all steam-driven machinery - the sudden stopping of high pressure steam demand from the boilers created a dangerous situation, so the pressure had to be relieved. There was nothing unusual about the noise - just that it was a bloody nuisance.

Little did I know that minutes later, escaping steam would be the *least* of my concerns.

Eleven

Help Required

Moments after Boxhall had left on his second inspection trip - the Carpenter appeared by my side in the enclosed bridge area. The overhead lighting had been switched-on so his features were very clear. Before he opened his mouth to speak, I could see that the news was dire.

His words came out in a torrent. In fact; he spoke so quickly that I had to tell him to stop and start again.

"Sorry sir" he apologised. "It is just that the news is not good at all.

I have sounded all the forward compartments including the most forward one - the Fore Peak Tank. Unfortunately; every starboard side compartment - from the bow to Boiler Room Five is making water. All of them - except Five - at a rapid rate. Five is filling very slowly."

As he finished speaking, a clerk from the ship's Post Office appeared behind him. The man was out of breath which told me I was about to receive even more dire news.

"I have to report, sir, that the Mail Room is rapidly filling with water and when I left a few minutes ago, the water had reached the second rung of the ladder leading up to the Sorting Room."

I had heard enough, and to emphasis the situation, I could now feel a decided lean of the ship over to the right - to the starboard side. Another quick check of the heel indicator confirmed this. We were in deep trouble - my lovely brand-new command was sinking.

Immediately, I ordered my First Officer to go forward and muster the Bosun and all hands on the boat deck and thereafter; to clear the lifeboats and have them ready for use.

Having issued my orders, I then told the 'messenger of doom' from the Mail Room:

"Right then! lad show me exactly what you are telling me!" and with that, I left the bridge and returned with the Mail Clerk below decks - I needed to see for myself!

On the way down, we met with the Chief Purser - a man named McIlroy and I told him to accompany us.

On arrival above the Mail Room, we did not hang about - it was too serious to waste any time! I told the Chief Purser to go to his Office, open the safe and bring the Official Papers and the Ship's Bag to the bridge. These valuable documents would need to come with us if we had to abandon ship. Besides which - the very latest details of the ship's movements would have been recorded in the Scrap Log Book and that had to come with us too. I then headed back to the bridge as quickly as I could.

By time I got back to the bridge, the entire ship was awake and wondering?

The stewards were busy comforting and reassuring

anxious passengers and Boxhall was awakening all the remaining officers.

When I was assured that all my orders were being carried-out, I headed for my Chart Room: I needed to find out where 'Titanic' was and thereafter - using the modern wonders of wireless - tell the world where we were and call for immediate assistance.

In my chart room I found a slip of paper containing details of the approximate position of 'Titanic' earlier that evening at 8 pm. I knew the direction of the track we had been following since 5-50pm when we turned at 'The Corner' and the patent log reading for 10 pm told me that due to the then flat calm conditions - 'Titanic' had indeed increased speed to 22.5 knots. All I then needed to calculate a distress position, was the time recorded in the Scrap Log.

With the foregoing ingredient, It took but a few minutes to calculate that position. It is emblazoned on my mind to this very day. It was: Latitude: 41- degrees, 44 minutes North - Longitude: 50 degrees 24 minutes West.

I wrote the distress position down on a scrap of paper. However, as I did so, I noted that the bridge clock was showing a time of close to midnight and the chronometer was showing a time of 03-15 GMT. Since it had been after Midnight on my own watch when I heard the engine room telegraphs ringing; this confirmed that the first part of the planned clock change had been made before we hit the ice.

Thereafter, I headed for the Marconi Wireless Room.

The Wireless Operators shared a sleeping cabin adjoining their place of work which contained their apparatus.

Normally; only one operator would be on duty at that time and the wireless duty Watch would not change until 2 am the following morning. However - when I arrived there, I found both of them awake.

Apparently; the Junior operator had agreed to relieve the senior 2 hours 24 minutes early. Two hours of that, were as a favour because the latter had been working overtime the previous evening and the remaining extra 24 minutes was part of the Junior's share of the planned clock set back. This confirmed yet again, that a partial clock change had taken place before we hit the ice.

Anyway! When I got there - the senior was getting ready for his bunk and the junior had already taken over and was was at his instrument. They were discussing the fact that the ship had stopped.

I was greeted by the Junior with: "May I help you sir?" To which I replied "yes - send this immediately" and handed him the slip of paper with the distress position written on it.

As I spoke, the senior of the two started putting his clothes back on and, with his feet still in carpet slippers, joined us. He immediately took over - asking: "Is this a distress sir?"

I replied "Yes! adding; "And be as quick as you can."

With these words, I left them to their task and headed back to my bridge - much had yet to be done!

Twelve

ALL HANDS ON DECK

When I got back to the bridge, it was just after midnight. The deck crew were arriving on the boat deck. 2nd Officer Lightoller arrived at the same time and was directing them to their duties. He was doing so with great difficulty since the steam from the boilers was still roaring out of the funnel vents and making normal spoken communications impossible. Despite this; the first boat had been cleared

It was obvious that in the absence of QM Olliver, who was away on messenger duties, Fourth Boxhall had called all Deck Officers, because they were coming on deck to supervise the boat preparations.

First Officer Murdoch was over on the (right)-port hand side of the boat deck and would be assisted by the Watch Navigators - Third Officer Pitman and Fifth Officer Lowe.

On the port (left) side -Second Officer Lightoller was being assisted by my Sixth Officer Moody. I needed Fourth Officer Boxhall with me on the bridge as a personal assistant.

Chief Officer Wilde had a roving Commission - his job

was to oversee the operations on both port and starboard boat decks and see that my orders were promptly obeyed.

Although the Lookouts were still up in the Crows Nest; my first instinct was to scan the horizon for sight of the lights of a potential rescue vessel. I did so, but alas! the horizon was clear and sharp and the only light I could see were those from stars and planets as they rose above the horizon to the eastward and dipped below it to the west.

As I continued to scan, the junior wireless Operator arrived by my side. He asked if we could do anything about the noise of escaping steam. I told him that I had already sent a Quartermaster with a message about it to the Chief Engineer and that the reply had been that it would be attended to as soon as possible.

As we shouted to each other the Chief fulfilled his promise and the fierce roar of escaping steam abruptly stopped. It was as though a giant door had been closed. At that moment, the world was full of shouted words emphasised by deathly silence. These were, in turn, abruptly cut-off as the hearing of those doing the shouting was restored.

Shortly after that, Boxhall returned to the bridge and asked me if he should calculate a distress position. I told him that I had already done so, using the approximate position of 'Titanic at 8 pm that evening. To my dismay - he told me that after he had worked the accurate position from Lightoller's extant observations for a time before 8 pm, he had found that the 8 pm approximate position was 20 miles in error. Consequently; the distress position I had calculated was also in error by that amount. I therefore agreed that he should calculate a more accurate distress position and take it to the wireless room immediately.

After Boxhall had left, I remembered where I had gone wrong when calculating my distress position.

Although Lightoller had obtained the true position of the ship by observation of the stars before 8 pm that evening; the calculations for obtaining that true position had not been completed by Boxhall until after 9 pm. Consequently instead of the 8 pm position having been a short extension of an earlier, true accurate position, it was simply a guess extended from an earlier guess of the 7-30 pm position made by a Junior Navigating Officer.

As Boxhall was returning from the wireless room after sending the amended distress signal, there was a loud cry of 'Lights!'. He immediately reached for the ship's telescope and scanned the horizon. Very quickly, he told me that he could see what seemed to him to be the white masthead light of a steamship. He guessed it was a steamship because only steamships carried white masthead lights.

However, one light was no clear indication. It may well have been a stern light or a fishing boat light. Additionally; there was no indication as to the direction in which the vessel showing it was traveling but all would become clear.

A few minutes later, Boxhall reported seeing a second white masthead light. It was located below and to the left of the first one seen. This comfirmed that the vessel showing these lights was a steamship and that she was approaching us. Additionally; that if she continued to do so - would pass down our port - left hand side.

Although this seemed to be the case; I was concerned that the vessel in question might not have wireless and be unaware of our plight and said so to Boxhall. He replied by suggesting that we should fire distress signals to get and hold the approaching vessel's attention and I agree with him.

As well as the conventional rocket-type signals; 'Titanic' had also been supplied with Socket Signals. These were dual-purpose, in that as well as acting like the conventional rocket - they were supplied in lieu of a gun or cannon which was also a Regulation day-time sound signals of distress. Additionally - these new signals rose to a height above the sea of almost double that of the conventional rockets.

We had been supplied with 36 of these projectiles - a box of 24 and one holding 12. They were stored on the bridge and the socket-barrels for firing them were mounted on the out side of the boat deck rail by the bridge-wing cabs. However; unlike the conventional rocket which was fired by lighting a fuse; these things were fired using a lanyard and friction detonator. The firing lanyard was stored in the box along with the projectiles but in accordance with the Carriage of Explosives Act, the friction detonators which were explosives in their own right, were kept separate in a secure magazine locker at the stern.

To fire these things, a projectile from the box was located in the firing tube -much like a muzzle - loading gun. Thereafter, a firing lanyard was attached to the pencil-like detonator and the detonator inserted down a centrally located tube in the projectile. A quick pull on the lanyard fired the detonator which in turn, fired the main charge sending the projectile skyward. At the top of its trajectory, the projectile exploded with an almighty 'BANG', while emitting a shower of bright white stars which floated gently seaward in the stillness that followed.

We needed detonators! so Boxhall entered the wheelhouse and telephoned the duty Quartermaster located at the stern and told him to bring both boxes of detonators to the bridge. I went out onto the boat deck to see how the preparations of the life boats were progressing. Meanwhile the approaching vessel got nearer and nearer.

A few minutes later; the young Junior Wireless Operator arrived by my side with a verbal report.

"Excuse me sir, I have to report that we have made contact with a German ship called 'Frankfurt'."

I asked him if he knew how far away she was and if she was coming to our assistance, but he could not tell me. I therefore told him to go and find out and let me know as soon as possible.

At that moment a man named Andrews arrived by my side and the young wireless man stood aside.

In those days, it was common practice for those building passenger vessels to place a Guarantee Team from the yard aboard a new vessel on her maiden voyage. In that way they could detect and in most cases, rectify small imperfections and if appropriate; recommend where necessary - improvements. Andrews headed such a team. Earlier, I had met him and -since he was a Naval Architect and knew 'Titanic' like the back of his hand - had asked him to verify my assessment as to whether 'Titanic' was doomed or not.

I dismissed the waiting wireless man and when the lad

had left, invited Andrews to join me in the wheelhouse, which by then, was empty. There; we would get a bit of privacy.

Andrews confirmed my worse fears and added to them by telling me that in his opinion, the vessel would be gone in a little over an hour and a half. He also told me that he had given the same information to our Chairman, Ismay.

Andrews had barely completed his report, when the young Wireless Operator returned. This time, he informed me that they had contact with the Cunard Line vessel 'Carpathia'.

Again I asked him where she was and if she was coming to our aid. To my annoyance and frustration - he once again replied that he did not know. There was only one thing for it - I had to go to the Wireless Room and find out for myself. I looked around - saw all was going to plan and after thanking Andrews, headed back to the Marconi Shack with the young fellow in tow. On the way, I saw our Chairman; young Mr Ismay - wearing a dressing gown and slippers, fussing about the boat deck like a mother hen Obviously, Andrews's latest news was having an effect. However, I had more pressing duties.

Back in the Wireless Room I found the senior man Phillips crouched over his apparatus with ear phones on his head... he was listening intently and held a hand up palm outward; indicating that he did not wish to be interrupted.

After a few moments, he sat back and removed the phones and told me that he had been in contact with our sister -ship, RMS Olympic and that her Wireless Operator had picked up our signals and was asking for more news.

I asked him where she was and he gave me her position. I also asked him if he had heard any more from 'Carpathia' and he told me her operator had just given him *her* position and that she had turned around and was heading for our position; adding that her captain had said he would be with us in four hours. He finished by handing me a slip of paper with the positions of 'Olympic' and 'Carpathia' written on it.

I quickly worked out the distances between us an these two and found that 'Carpathia' was by far the nearest and would be with us as her captain had indicated - by daylight. Whereas, 'Olympic' was more than 500 miles away and would not be with us before the next evening at the earliest. Our situation was desperate!

When I returned to the bridge, I found Boxhall, the Purser and his Assistant waiting for me.

Boxhall reported that he had sent for the signal detonators and that the Quartermaster had reported seeing a lifeboat off our starboard side. I sent him to find out who had issued such an order, then I turned to the Pursers.

As ordered, my Head Purser Mr McIlroy had brought the ship's bag, I had a look inside - saw that it contained the Official Log Book and the ship's papers and then added the Scrap Log Book to it. I told McIlroy to take it along to Chief Officer Murdoch and tell him to have the bag put in a lifeboat at a convenient moment. A few minutes later - young Pitman and Boxhall arrived back on the bridge.

Boxhall confirmed that he had spoken with First Officer

Murdoch and that the latter told him he had been bullied into filling and launching a lifeboat by Chairman Ismay.

Young Pitman confirmed that Ismay was once again using his authority to bully him into loading and launching *his* Lifeboat, but that he had preferred to get the order directly from me.

By this time, 'Titanic' was noticeably down by the bows and starting to list to the left...port side. I could sense that things might be getting out of hand, so I told Pitman to go ahead and load his boat and launch it. Just then, Two Quartermasters arrived from the stern with the detonators for firing the distress signals.

Meanwhile; Boxhall had gone out onto the port - left - wing of the bridge and was studying the approaching vessel through his binoculars.

By then, I didn't need binoculars - the vessel was now much nearer and less than ten miles away because I could now see his two white mast head lights clearly with the naked eye.

As I had thought and Boxhall had predicted - she was on a course that would bring her down our port side and very soon her red side light would be visible with the naked eye.

As I studied this approaching vessel, it occurred to me that she must be one of the many all over the oceans who were yet to be fitted with wireless equipment. Otherwise-our wireless distress signal would almost have blasted the eardrums of her operator.

Boxhall sensed my presence beside him and asked if he should begin firing the socket distress signals. I answered in the affirmative and also ordered him to use our powerful Morse Signaling Light to reinforce the attempt to contact her and keep her attention. Fortunately; one of the Quartermasters had been a signaler in the Royal Navy so could easily attend to that task. I told them to tell the nearby vessel that we were sinking and in need of immediate assistance.

Under The Regulations, rocket signals were to be fired at short intervals of a few minutes to indicate urgency - to draw and hold the attention of a potential rescuer. However we agreed that since we could already see our potential savior and doubtless they could see us - the exact intervals of firing were less important than the act of getting and holding their attention and establishing inter-communication.

I was suddenly aware that Boxhall was talking to me... "Shall I start firing the signals, Sir?"

I replied that he may as well do so. My watch showed 00-40 am.

Five minutes later, there was a loud bang on the starboard side as they fired the first projectile sky-ward. Seconds later there was a second, much louder ear-splitting bang - this time; high in the sky just off our starboard side.

Instantly: a ball of brilliant white stars bust hundreds of feet up - illuminating 'Titanic' as if in day light. It would have been impossible for those in the approaching ship not to have seen it!

During the chilling silence that followed - the pyrotechnic stars slowly drifted down like fire-feathers and were extinguished one by one. Unless the sailors in the approaching ship were sleeping, blind or even deaf - that phenomenon could never have been missed by them

However, that spectacular pyrotechnic display was very much noticed by all those on and around the decks of 'Titanic'. Suddenly, there was an urgency which until then appeared to be absent. This had become real!

The boat decks were becoming busier by the moment. Passengers were gathering and standing around in knots- all of them obviously looking for guidance. Members of the catering and engine room crews were appearing among them. However everyone was well behaved and orderly. Despite all this, there was little or no conversation... it was very strange indeed!

Shortly after that first signal, Chief Officer Wilde and Second Officer Lightoller arrived by my side.

Wilde was anxious about the lifeboat loading program and the trim of the ship. His concern was that the increase in the top weight caused by the number of people on the upper decks and removal of weight from one side due to filling and launching of boats would cause 'Titanic' to lean over to the left.

Lightoller had heard about the boats being loaded and launched on the starboard side and wished to know if he should start loading boats on *his* side. In addition - for some reason or other - he wanted to know if he should embark women and children first.

I thought about that second question for a moment or two and then agreed that he should go ahead and do so. Incidentally: I had several reasons for this.

First: the women and children were less suited to lending physical help that were the men. They were inappropriately dressed and less physically able to board the boats in the normal way which was by ladder using the ship's gangway doors. But most important of all: the method of lowering the boats was by a single rope slackened around a deck fixture at each end of the boat. This meant that if each rope was slackened evenly - each would bear half the weight of the boat and its contents. However, if one rope became jammed; the shock-load imposed on it would be less in a lighter-loaded boat and consequently the rope would be less likely to break and spill its contents into the sea far below.

Another 'bang' and another signal soared high above our heads to explode in a shower of stars like its predecessor. Yet again; this was ignored by the approaching vessel whose red side light was now visible to the naked eye. This last being confirmed by young Lowe, my Fifth Officer who was working nearby on one of the starboard side lifeboats.

Soon; lifeboats 7, 5, 3 and 1 had been filled and sent away from the forward starboard, right hand, side of the boat deck and the weight was now unevenly distributed - it being concentrated on the port, left-hand side. It was about this time that I noticed that 'Titanic' was now leaning over to port. I remembered the concerns of my Chief Officer... his concerns had become a reality!

Apart from the danger of turning over; a no less dangerous result of this would be difficulty for those trying to get into the lifeboats on that side. Many would have to jump across a gap caused by the boats hanging vertically.

There were two ways to solve the problems. These were:

one - to move all those gathered on the port side across to the starboard side and bring the ship upright once again and two: at the same time - temporarily cease loading boats on the starboard side and thereafter, concentrate on the port side. Consequently; I found Chief Officer Wilde and outlined my plans. Thereafter; he began herding all surplus persons on the port side of the decks, over to the starboard side. He was a big lad and had a big voice to match. With the aid of a megaphone, he completed moving people in a very short space of time.

I assisted in lowering a couple of boats myself.

First: I helped lower boats on the port side of the boat decks. I think these were boats numbered 8 and 6. The latter was situated on the port side outside the entrance to the Officer's Quarters. I remember this one in particular because I had it lowered to the deck below which was 'A' Deck, but forgot that unlike the 'Olympic', our 'A' Deck was enclosed and there were windows in the way of people trying to board a boat from the forward end of that deck.

Bang! Yet another signal exploded above our heads and yet again, it was ignored by the nearby vessel which seemed to be slowing down...had he seen us at last? Not a chance! In fact he continued to ignore us and just after that; turned away to the westward and showed us his white stern light. By the line of the horizon, I reckoned he was no more than six miles away when he did that. However, he did not sail away, but seemed to stop at that time. There was only one other thing we could do. Using my megaphone, I ordered those manning the lifeboats to row across to that vessel, report our plight; land the survivors and come back for more. In that way we could ferry as many people as possible in the limited time available before 'Titanic' sank.

I decided to go over to the starboard side and see what was going on over there. As I passed through the bridge, I heard the telephone sounding in the wheel house. At that time the area was clear of people and I knew everyone was otherwise engaged, so I went and answered. It was the Chief Engineer. He sounded extremely agitated.

"The news is not good, sir" he reported. "All the available pumps are working full-out but the water is continuing to rise. Boiler room six is now almost completely flooded and the watertight doors are closed. Boiler Room Five was holed in the forward bunker and we closed the bunker doors, but they have now given-way and 5 is also filling. The water tight doors to these compartments are still tight -shut. Now its getting in to boiler room four. I don't know how much longer we can stay down here."

The man had done his level best and could do no more. I told him to send up all non essential officers and crew - make things safe, then get out of there himself. I then headed back to the wireless room.

In the wireless room, I found the senior man still crouched over his apparatus. I waited until he had finished what he was working on then asked for the latest situation.

He told me that besides the 'Carpathia' there were now three more ships heading for our location. These were a Canadian Pacific vessel named 'Mount Temple', our own 'Olympic' and he had just heard from the German vessel

'Frankfurt' which had been the first one to answer his calls. She too was now heading in our direction.

I compared the positions of these ships and decided that 'Carpathia' was still the nearest and would arrive as I thought - at about 4-30pm - just as dawn was breaking. I told him to tell the captain of 'Carpathgia' that we were putting the women in the life boats and that the water was up to the boilers and the engine room would soon be flooded.

When I had finished, I looked at the wireless room Clocks - there were two of them. One showed Eastern Standard Time at New York and the other partly adjusted ship time. The first read 11-38 pm and the other; 1-13 am, April 15.

As I left, the operator was already sending the latest information over the air waves.

Back on the bridge, I had an up-dated report from Boxhall. He told me that he had fired another signal and although the nearby vessel was still in the position in which she had stopped - all attempts to contact her had failed.

By this time - 'Titanic's' bow was well down and I could see that the sea was beginning to wash across the forward well-deck and about to over-top the door-step and enter into the forecastle accommodation. Now - the act of walking across the boat deck was an increasing effort. The end was not far off!

I told Boxhall to stop doing what he was doing and accompany me to the port side of the bridge.

When we arrived on the port side, the filling of boats

was in full swing. I noticed that Emergency Boat 2 was still hanging in her davits but had been filled with women and children and was ready to go, so I told Boxhall to take command of her. He protested - pointing out that there were still many signals left in the boxes. I told him to forget about them and that the Quartermaster could easily attend to them if required.

Reluctantly he agreed, but before obeying my order, he quickly went back into the enclosed bridge and almost immediately returned with a box of Company Signals. These were hand held, green-coloured pyrotechnics used for identification and communicating with other Company vessels at night. He chucked these into the boat and quickly followed them. I didn't bother to question him about them.

A few minutes later, Wilde was by my side and we ordered the able seamen manning the lowering ropes (falls) at each end of the boat to start slackening. Immediately the boat began to descend toward the sea - the heads of its seated passengers disappeared below the boat deck rail.

Suddenly there was a cry from the boat! They informed me that there were not enough able bodied men to row it once it was afloat.

I ordered the men to stop lowering and looked around but apart from a few men passengers, the deck was empty. Then one of them who had heard that cry came forward and offered his services. I recognised him. He was one of the First Class passengers - a Canadian military man. Earlier, he had been assisting with clearing the boats. He assured me that he was very familiar with things maritime, so I permitted him to slide down into the boat using one of the boat's man-ropes. Thereafter, the boat was lowered safely and efficiently to the sea and left the ship's side without problems.

Shortly after this, there was yet another bang- the Quartermaster who had been assisting Boxhall had fired another signal. I had almost forgotten about him!

I hurried over to the other side and as I left the enclosed bridge area, met him returning to the wheelhouse to replace the firing lanyard. He was about to return to the Morse Light sending key when I told him that he should stop there and then - that Boxhall had left and that he should go and assist with the preparation and launch of our collapsible boats.

We had four collapsible boats - one each side on top of the bridge housing and one each side on the boat deck. These were a new fangled idea. Each boat had a standard lifeboat style lower hull made of wood and collapsible canvas sides which were raised and secured in place when in use. To fill and launch them, they were re-located under the emergency boat davits and attached to them after the emergency boats had been launched.

Around about that time, I remembered the wireless men in their workplace. In the rush of the previous actions I had almost forgotten about them too. I headed for the Wireless Room.

In the wireless room, the two operators were having trouble with the power. They told me that they had had to switch over to emergency battery power. I could well understand their problem.

Although the ship's lights were still burning brightly;

they had flickering and dimming a few times. I inwardly hoped they would last until the end.

The lads told me that they were still in touch with the 'Carpathia' and that her wireless signals were still being received loud and clear.

I thanked them for their devotion to duty but felt that I had to tell them that the end was fast approaching. Consequently I told them to secure their apparatus, shut it down and head for the remaining boats. Suddenly! I remembered that I needed to show an example by putting-on my own life jacket which was still on the bridge, and so I headed in that direction.

On my way back, I noticed that the ships bow was even farther down, but the slope remained much the same. It crossed my mind that a goodly chunk of my ship was now suspended high out of the water in an alien environment without any form of support. It was also the 'heavy end' of the ship containing the engines and machinery... something had to give - and soon!

The bridge was almost deserted except for those struggling with the two remaining collapsible boats... the other two had been launched in my absence.

As I stood there, the two wireless men came out onto the port side of the boat deck. The younger one came forward to help Lightoller and others with the Collapsible remaining on the top of the deck house on that side. On the other hand - his senior simply turned and began walking up the sloping boat deck toward the stern.

I continued over to the other side of the bridge and

found Murdoch and Wilde aided by a passenger and a few seamen trying to get the other Collapsible down off the cabin roof. They had constructed a sort of skid, using oars and were about to slide it down them. There was nothing I could do to help, so I made my way into the covered area to fetch my life jacket and a few personal effects. I had just done so and was leaving by the port side door when there was a loud report and a distinct twisting feeling. This was followed by a second report.

At that same moment, the bow took a dive downward and I was washed out of and over the port bridge wing by the overwhelming Atlantic Ocean.

So there you have it my friends. You know what followed and we're back where I started this tale. Thank you for listening to my ramblings; and now -do you have any questions?

PART TWO

Thirteen

ANY QUESTIONS?

"You must admit, sir, that your story is a hard one to swallow. However, setting that aside - can we assume that since your miraculous reincarnation and our subsequent arrival here, that you have been able to read and view the plethora of material that has been written and filmed about the 'Titanic'? If so - do you have any observation to make concerning any of these?"

I answered them in the affirmative; confirming that I had also read all the transcripts of evidence given by survivors on both sides of the Atlantic, as well as the official findings in each case.

I also pointed out to them that having done so, my opinion was that the whole story of that dreadful disaster had been tainted by press hysteria, political expediency, lies and romantic inaccuracies. Beginning with the Official Inquiries which I told them (and believe to this day) had been a travesty of justice. Not only in the way they had portrayed me, but how they had conducted the proceedings and how they had treated the memory of other brave men thereafter.

I finished by telling them them that the very reason why they were sitting there was because I had brought myself up-to date with what the world believed regarding the events leading up to and including the loss of RMS Titanic and that I now wanted to set the record straight. Once more, I asked them: "Now where do you want me to start?"

They replied as one -

"We suggest at the beginning - when 'Titanic' was handed over at Belfast and sailed around to Southampton".

"So be it!" I told them. In fact; I anticipated this and have prepared a list of notes, for you. These are of inaccuracies as I recall them.

Fourteen

THE INACCURACIES

Inaccuracy Number One.
The Arrival time on the Delivery Trip from Belfast to Southampton Southampton.

I read that 'Titanic' arrived at Southampton at Midnight on April 14 and was berthed at that time. That cannot be true!

The problem here is that non mariners do not appreciate that technically; a vessel has no less than three 'Arrival' times.

The first arrival time is known as 'End of Passage'. This is when the ship arrives at the Pilot Station at her destination and the engines are put on stand-by ready for maneuvering if necessary.

The second 'Arrival Time' is when under the guidance of the Pilot, the ship enters the Port Authority jurisdiction.

The third 'Arrival Time' is when the captain rings down 'Finished with engines.' That is when the tugs are let go when securely at anchor or when the last rope is made fast to the shore. In other words - when engine power is no longer needed and when the vessel is secured at her berth.

In the case of 'Titanic'; the passage from Belfast commenced when the pilot left us north of Grey Point around 8-30 pm that evening. That was after sea trials had been completed. It ended around 11-40 pm the following evening when we stopped to pickup the pilot at The Nabb.

Lightoller was First Officer on that trip and he told his questioners that she had averaged 18 knots. We can verify that!

From 8-30 pm Full Away on Passage to 11-40 pm End of Passage the following evening is 27 hours 10 minutes on passage which, multiplied by the average speed of 18 knots, equates to a total distance of 488 miles. The Pilot Book measured distance from Belfast pilot to Southampton pilot is recorded as 492 miles so Lightoller wasn't too far out.

From end of passage and after stopping to pick up the Pilot; we had another 5 miles to steam up channel to the Southampton port limits and we got there around 1 pm on the morning of April 4. In fact, you will find that time recorded in the Southampton Archives.

From there, we had a narrow channel passage up to the White Star Dock where we made fast the tugs in preparation to turn the ship and enter the dock stern-first. In fact - it was daylight by the time we made fast the last rope and were finished with engines and tugs.

So you can see, it was a physical impossibility for 'Titanic' to have arrived at her berth at midnight if she arrived at the pilot station at 20 minutes to midnight. The total distance was near to 535 nautical miles. To arrive at that time in 27.1 hours 'Titanic' would have to have averaged almost 20 knots and she never got close to that except for a couple of hours around 6 am that morning when the engineers increased the engine revolutions for a brief trial. Even then... they would not have been permitted to run them at maximum design revolutions. That would have been absurd and might have meant us turning around and heading back to Belfast for repairs. Add to that the fact that she was continuously in Tidal waters with strong currents... not a good area for engine speed trials.

Inaccuracy - Number Two
'We were trying to beat the Atlantic crossing time of our sister-ship RMS Olympic.'

This idea - like all of the inaccuracies written about that fateful voyage - obviously arose in the mind or minds of a person or persons who has/have no first-hand knowledge of how a new vessel is treated on her maiden voyage, or of the detailed planning that goes into the scheduling of the voyage of an Ocean-going Passenger Liner or of the voyage-planning of any passenger ship for that matter.

Passenger Vessel Companies - just like Train Companies, use pre-published Time Tables. Potential passenger consult these and plan their journey accordingly. Obviously; any Company that did not run its transport to a pre-published Time Table would very soon get a bad reputation.

If we had Run 'Titanic' to beat a record, it would mean that we had disregarded our Time Table and ignored the plans of our fare-paying passengers - those who used it.

We would have arrived at our destination earlier than planned - used more fuel than had been planned and incurred higher berthing fees than planned. Because; we would also have third party problems with essential services needed to dock.

Pilots, Tugs and Harbour personnel are booked in advance and based on the published Time Table- particularly in a busy port like New York. Consequently; passenger liners don't arrive when they feel like it!

Apart from the foregoing: A new ship has brand new engines - each with multiple moving parts. Any engineer will tell you that back then, engines had to be run-in'.

In other words - all moving parts had to be gradually loaded over a minimum time to avoid sudden failure. Such a failure on a maiden voyage could be catastrophic at the worst but would in any case - involve a trip back to the builder's yard, causing serious delays and a huge loss in revenue and reputation. As a result of the foregoing; we ran 'Titanic' at a moderate speed up until Noon on April 14. In fact; when I calculated the amount of clock change between April 14 and April 15; I did not allow for an increase in distance between these two Noons and consequently I had no plans to increase speed. In fact, the plan thereafter, was to increase the revolutions by a small amount for the remaining voyage time days and adjusting them to ensure that we arrived at New York on time, as planned and per Time Table - on April 17. Additionally; we were crossing the North Atlantic in Spring time - a time notorious for delays due to fog close the the North American mainland. Consequently; we had to take that into consideration as well.

Inaccuracy Number Three
Messages & Ice Reports.

Earlier I mentioned messages received by me. Here they are... I wrote them down.

From the SS Caronia April 14:

"Captain, 'Titanic.' - Westbound steamers report bergs, growlers and field ice in 42° N. from 49° to 51° W., 12th April. Compliments. - Barr.'

This one was obviously a courtesy message since the ice information was second hand and referred to the historic position of ice lying along the 42nd parallel of latitude two days earlier.

Like most captains... Barr knew that the ships who reported that ice were on an East-West course and that sea ice in that area normally moved north and mainly eastward.

He also knew the approximate position of 'Titanic' that morning and that that I could never have sighted the ice in question before I reached the position where ships like us turned toward New York.

Then we have one from one of our own White Star ships - the RMS Baltic. It read:

'Capt. SMITH, Titanic:

Have had moderate variable winds and clear fine weather since leaving. Greek steamer 'Athinai' reports passing icebergs and large quantity of field ice today in latitude 41.51 north, longitude 49.52 west. Last night we spoke German oil tank Deutschland, Stettin to Philadelphia, not under control; short of coal; latitude 40.42 north, longitude 55.11. Wishes to be reported to New York.'

This was yet again; another second-hand information and related to the sighting of ice in the same area as the ice mentioned in the 'Caronia' message. I gave to Ismay and retrieved from him later. I did so because it was from one of our own ships.

Ismay noted the word ice and asked me about it. I told him it was of little concern to us since it referred to ice way to the north of our intended track and was more or less in the same position as the ice mentioned two days earlier in the 'Caronia' message.

Finally we had the one overheard from the 'Californian' to the 'Antillian'.

Unlike the previous two - this one was a proper ice - specific warning of a first-hand sighting of ice ice which was a potential danger to one of 'Californian's' own Company vessels. It was relevant to the 'Antillian' because she was following the same track as was the 'Californian'...a track which followed the 42nd parallel of latitude.

"To Captain, 'Antillian,' 6.30 pm. apparent ship's time; lat. 42° 3' N., long. 49° 9' W. Three large bergs five miles to southward of us. Regards. - Lord."

I reiterate: the foregoing message was a dedicated. properly phrased 'Ice Report' but it was not addressed to 'Titanic'. In fact, I have since learned that it was by sheer accident that my Junior Wireless Operator picked-up that message. I do not recall ever setting eyes on it but can only assume that since it was informal, it was simply included in his report to the bridge when he went off duty at 8pm that evening. However, even if I did sight it, I would have concluded that the ice in question was part of the same ice mentioned in the previous two general messages which contained reference to ice - ice that would not be considered a threat to my ship since it was well north of my planned track.

You should understand that I had been crossing the Atlantic for many years before this and - like all other captains who had done the same thing - knew that the ice in question would normally have been moving under the influence of the West Wind Drift - which is the eastern extension of the Gulf Stream; This means that it normally moved in an Easterly direction at a rate of between a half and one knot. In other words... constantly getting farther and farther away from where 'Titanic' would be and consequently, no danger to us at all.

As I said earlier: the main reason I showed Ismay the 'Baltic' message was that it came from the captain of one of our own Company Ships and he would appreciate being shown it. Otherwise; there would have been no point in doing so since he was not a Navigator, so the co-ordinate numbers relative to ice would have no meaning to him.

Inaccuracy Number Four
Average speed from Noon, April 14.

I have read that the declared average speed of 'Titanic' from Noon, April 14 until she hit the ice berg was 22.4 knots. That is simply not true and here is why....

Oh sorry! Before going any farther, I'll explain a few basic facts about measuring speed at sea and how we dealt with changes in time. I'll try not to be too technical.

If there is anything that needs clarifying - please ask, but basically; this how we estimated speed when we did not know exactly where we were.

Back in 1912, there were two methods of determining a ships' speed. The first was the ancient method used on sailing ships called The Log. So called because it derived its name from the practice of throwing a wooden log over the side on a rope with a knot in it and timing the moment when the knot passed over the rail...i.e. 1 knot. Not to be confused with 'The Official Log Book'!

However, the advent of the propeller brought another method whereby o. One revolution was equal to the distance the propeller traveled through the water after turning once. Thus, the number of revolutions turned in one hour equaled the distance traveled in that hour, hence the speed of the ship.

Our modern young officers were divided as to which method they preferred. Second Officer Boxhall liked speed by revolutions. However, Young Fifth Officer Lowe - like me - preferred the traditional method. I must add; by then we had advanced from the knot in the rope system.

On 'Titanic' we had the very latest, accurate Patent Log.

A Patent Log was a device which measured the distance traveled by a ship every hour and hence an accurate indication of her speed over that particular hour.

Basically: it consisted of a 'spinner'- a propeller-like device which was attached to the end of a long rope trailed behind the moving ship.

The ship-end of the rope was attached to a nautical mile-counting device mounted on the side-rail at the stern, In practice; that device registered the number of times the spinner rotated. It worked in much the same way as does the speedometer on a motor car.

For every one nautical mile, the 'spinner' rotated exactly 9000 times. This meant that the faster it spun during one hour - the more knots were shown on the 'mile counter' or register dial.

Every day at 12 o' clock Noon, the Patent Log of 'Titanic' - as on all other ships - was set to zero. Thereafter; it was read every two hours by a Quartermaster and the results telephoned to the Navigation Bridge and recorded in the log book.

Basically; we then had a distance traveled over a fixed time. By dividing the first by the second, we got an average speed.

Here is an example of what happened the day before the disaster.

At 12 o' clock Noon by the bridge clock on April 13, the Patent Log read 519 nautical miles. The indicator hands, which were much like the hands of a clock, were then set to zero.

After this was done, it was calculated that for the bridge clock to read 12 o'clock Noon the next day, April 14, it would have to be set back a total of 44 minutes and as normal; this was done at Midnight that night.

At 12 Noon April 14, the Patent Log was read. This time, it showed 546.5 miles.

Since, the ship's clocks had been retarded 44 minutes at Midnight, April 13, this meant that the ship had been running 24 hours 44 minutes since the last time when the Patent Log had been set to zero. During that time we had covered a distance of 546.1 miles. Dividing that total difference between Noon 13 reading and Noon 14 readings by that Day's Run-time of 24 hours 44 minutes gave me the average speed for that day. It was 22.1 knots.

As I mentioned before; going west we retarded the ship's clock each day, Consequently; when all the other calculations had been made and the Noon, April 14 position calculated, I then had to decide how many minutes we needed to retard the clock between bridge time Noon, April 14 and bridge time the next day - Noon, April 15. To do this, I had to make an estimate of the Longitude of 'Titanic' at bridge time Noon the next day - April 15. That would be when the sun would be due south of the ship's position.

I knew that we had about 126 miles to run on the course we were steering at that time, before turning more to the west - and when we did so. would be increasing the rate of change of westerly longitude. This would happen at the time of 5-50pm that afternoon.

I also knew that I had no intention of increasing speed before Noon the next day, so I set-to work

My calculations told me that the next Day's Run from Noon April 14 to Noon April 15 would be 24 hours 47 minutes... 3 minutes longer than the previous Day's Run. As with all such adjustments to a ship's bridge clocks, this would be done at night, which meant that everyone on the ship got 47 minutes extra sleep or - if on duty - 47 minutes extra work.

The extra working time was shared between the 8 to Midnight Duty Watch and the following Midnight to 4 am Duty Watch. This meant that between April 13 and April 14; each Duty Watch shared the extra 47 minutes work time. Whereas, the remaining members of the crew and passengers would get the benefit of an extra 47 minutes in bed. If there was an unequal number of extra minutes of a planned clock change, the junior 8 to Midnight Watch would take the lion's share of extra work time.

As I told you before - I was very familiar with that part of the Atlantic Ocean and expected to meet a head current that afternoon of April 14. This, I calculated, would slow 'Titanic' down by about half a knot...to 21.5 knots

As planned - we turned onto our final track for New York at 5-50pm and ten minutes later - at 6pm - the Quartermaster sent us the Patent Log reading...it was 125.7 miles. Dividing this by the run time of 6 hours from Noon, confirmed my expectations regarding a head-current slowing us down. Instead of keeping-up the pre-noon average speed of 22.1 knots, we had only averaged 20.95 knots. More than a full knot slower!

I seem to remember a log reading of 162 miles but I think that was around 7-35 pm. If so, it would have been called for by the junior Navigator to be used in calculating an approximate position for the pending star sight calculations by Lightoller to establish a true position.

However, I do remember that the Patent Log reading

sent up to the bridge just after hitting the iceberg was 260 nautical miles. This is where we find difficulty in reconciling the popularly accepted average speed and the true average speed that afternoon and evening.

I said that the Patent Log reading at 6 pm was 125.7 nautical miles. Subtracting that from 260 gives a difference of 134.3 miles.

It is claimed that the clocks were not altered before hitting the ice, if so, then the run time between 6 pm and the moment of hitting the ice would be 5 hours 40 minutes which equates to an average speed of 24 knots, which is absurd. On the other hand - if a partial clock change set-back of 24 minutes had been made just before hitting the ice, the run time between 6 pm and hitting the ice would have been 6 hours 04 minutes which equates to an average speed of 22.1 knots.

From surviving witness statement, we know that the ship averaged 22.5 knots by patent Log from 8 pm that evening. This means that of the total of 134.3 miles steamed between 6 pm and the moment of hitting the iceberg, 91.5 of them were covered from 8pm until the moment of impact. The remaining 42.8 miles were covered between 6pm and 8pm at an average speed of 21.4 knots. All of which, proves beyond reasonable doubt that a partial clock change took place just before we hit that damned iceberg.

Don't take my word for all of this; there is a less complicated way of proving that a partial clock change took place.

The absolute proof comes from the evidence of the surviving members of the 8 to Midnight and Midnight to

4am Working Watches who shared that 24 minute partial clock change.

In their evidence, the Lookouts Fleet and Lee in the Crows Nest at the time of hitting the iceberg, very clearly stated that 8 bells were sounded signifying Midnight - the end of the Watch. These were not only a clock time but a clear indication that the Duty Watch had completed their total allocated working time which in the case of the Lookouts, was 2 hours 24 minutes.

Corroboration came from the lookouts taking over from Fleet and Lee. They said they did so about 20 minutes after hitting the iceberg.

You should know that the sound of 8 bells is not only a ship time, but they are also a signal... a signal indicating the end of a duty period. In this case... the duty period was 4 hours 24 minutes.

Basically; the inaccuracy concerning average speed that night is due to a lack of understanding of the sworn evidence, which in turn, is caused by a lack of knowledge as to how the bridge of a British Merchant ship worked back in my day.

Fifteen

MORE INACCURACIES

<u>Inaccuracy Number Five</u>
<u>The helm orders and the bow swing.</u>

I am amazed at the lack of understanding regarding ship-handling and propeller behaviour illustrated in the plethora of books, articles, motion pictures and television documentaries depicting how it happened that morning.

I have read and seen that everyone thinks that when poor Murdoch first saw the iceberg he ordered hard a starboard (hard left) and full astern on the engines, immediately followed by hard-a-port (hard right) on the helm, and that afterward, he told me that he had intended to go to port around it but that it was too late and she struck.

In fact, Murdoch simply told me he intended to avoid the iceberg by going round it to the left, but he had no time to do so - that it was too close and we hit the damn thing.

I suspect the problem is a misunderstanding in the use of the English words- 'round' and 'around'.

All three Quartermasters on duty at the time of the accident survived.

The man steering the ship - QM Hichens very clearly stated in his evidence that Murdoch told him to put the helm hard-left but just as Hichens got the steering-wheel over to that position, she hit the ice and Murdoch rushed to the engines - nothing more! He also vehemently stated at both Inquiries that he received a single hard-left helm order from Murdoch during the attempt to avoid the ice.

On the other hand, his Watch Mate, QM Olliver clearly stated that a second helm order was indeed given, but not until the iceberg was at the stern and clear of the ship. That would have been at least half a minute after the first helm order.

At that moment his other Watch mate QM Rowe was at the stern. He confirmed that the iceberg was about 10 feet out from the ship as it passed him. However a first class passenger saw it from his cabin port-hole as it passed the bridge and said that at that time, it was about 50 feet out from the ship's side. His evidence, coupled with that of QM Rowe shows that 'Titanic' was closing with the ice berg and still under hard left rudder, 30 seconds after it had been first applied and after the ice had passed astern. This being so - why on earth would Murdoch have given a reverse helm order so late in the day? Absolute nonsense!

QM Hichens also stated that after receiving his orders and applying the helm, 'Titanic's bow swung to the left - changing the direction it was pointing- by 22.5 degrees... the famous 'two points'. That was where the fairy-tales and the judicial pressure began!

To simulate the evidence using a similar vessel; the RMS Olympic, was commandeered to emulate that two- point - 22.5 degree turn and then assess the results.

This was as much use as a chocolate sailor in the desert!

For a start off; at the beginning of the simulation, everyone was ready for the order... there would have been no delay in execution and worst of all - the speed used was 18 knots - 4.5 knots slower than the real thing.

The result was that it took 'Olympic' 37 second from initial order to completion of the turn.

From that simple statistic; judiciary and authors compiled the most ridiculous collection of nonsensical tales in the annals of marine history.

To begin with: Hichens - the quartermaster steering the ship very clearly stated at both Inquiries into the disaster that the time from the initial helm order to the moment of hitting the ice - when 'Titanic' was on her original course - until she hit - took as long as it took for him to turn the steering-wheel full- over. The standard time for a professional, experienced helmsman to complete such an order was 5 or 6 seconds. This is confirmed in Seamanship Manuals of the time. Therefore that is how long 'Titanic' was off her original course before she hit the ice - not 37 seconds as suggested by that daft experiment.

Yet; in the motion picture 'Titanic' the viewer clearly sees the order given and hears the actor playing the Helmsman asking.. 'Why isn't she turning'.

However, there's more!

Subsequent authors took that 37 seconds delay and the second helm order and cooked them into a story which has been accepted by many over the ensuing years.

It has been claimed that in order to avoid the iceberg, my First Officer Murdoch performed and completed a zig - zag manoeuvre, whereby he first ordered the helm hard left then immediately thereafter, hard right. As you have seen; the evidence tells us that was clearly not the case!

First of all: a man of Murdoch's experience would never have touched the engines had he intended such an action. Because he knew that full engine power and consequently full volume propeller-wash (particularly in a vessel with a central propeller) over the rudder surfaces are essential for maximum rudder efficiency which would have been necessary for such a manoeuvre at that time.

However, others have exploited the foregoing and the 37 turning time experiment results even farther by linking them to another subject which is also full of inaccuracies. By this, I mean the separate story linking the SS Californian with the disaster. I will deal with that later but first - this 2 point turn anomaly.

As we have seen; the Quartermaster stated that the ship turned two points and that gave birth to the turn experiment.

However; a fact concerning the interaction between a fast moving ship and a relatively stationary object has been completely overlooked. Allow me to explain.

When a ship is moving in a straight line, her center of gravity - like that of all moving objects is at the center- line of the vessel. However; if she strikes something directly in line with that center, she will do one of two things: (1) stop and crush her bow or (2) stop and bounce off it. However; if any part of her bow areas strike such an object off - center, that ship will swing toward the first point of contact and her stern on the same side will swing away from it. Such was the case with 'Titanic'!

When her starboard 'shoulder' which was moving at 22.5 knots, heavily brushed against that iceberg, the starboard side was partially impeded. This caused the bow to swing toward - not away- from the ice. However; because of the speed and the rudder action; as her bow passed the obstruction, she quickly came under the influence of the rudder once again and she broke loose from the ice - just past the bridge on the starboard side - and resumed her left hand turn. However; by that time, the engines were slowing... the center propeller had stopped and the turn was rapidly slowing down.

When I asked Hichens how her head was, he told me it was about West-south-West.. In short - the bow had initially and quickly swung two points to starboard and then finally - back two points to port.

As for the second helm and engine orders? I gave these myself and that was some time after the first set. By then, the ship was more or less stopped dead in the water pointing West-south-West. In other words; she had change her original heading by two points to port.

At that time, I did not think we were damaged much at all, so I decided to bring our bow back to point in the direction of New York, and be ready to resume the voyage as soon as as I got the expected 'all-clear' report from my Carpenter and those doing the damage inspections. To this effect, I ordered a quick burst of power ahead and at the same time...hard-a- port (hard right) on the rudder.

As soon as her bow started swinging right, I stopped the engines and had the helmsman steady the bow pointing in the direction of our original course. Then I waited for the results of the damage inspection.

Four minutes later, I received the reports of the Carpenter and the Mail Clerk and I had to reconsider the position we seemed to be in.

At that moment, 'Titanic' was heading on her original course - not northward as concocted in various stories since then. In fact, the evidence of my 3rd Officer Pitman; given at the American Inquiry, very clearly pointed that out when he told them he headed north from the right hand starboard side of the ship in life boat number 5.

Inaccuracy Number Six.
The sighting of an Approaching Vessel

Among many of the things that irritate me about the modern version of the story of my ship, is the frequent ignoring of swathes of sworn evidence by officialdom on both sides of the Atlantic, aggravated by subsequent so called 'experts'. In this case I refer to evidence concerning the moving ship seen from 'Titanic' by me and other witnesses, including young Joe Boxhall.

As I told you - when first we stopped after hitting the iceberg, there was no great concern - I thought we had been lucky. However, as I also told you; that comfort soon came to an end. In fact; ten minutes after we stopped to be precise. That was the moment when I knew or suspected that we were going to sink and it was not a matter of 'if' but 'when'.

I was not the only one who had those thoughts; very many of my crew and in particular, the Lookouts in the Crows Nest, were aware of it. More so when the Deck Crew started clearing the life boats fifteen minutes after we stopped.

This being the situation: I ask you: do any of you, or anyone else for that matter, seriously think that anyone in their right mind - finding them self in such a perilous situation - particularly the lads in the Crow's Nest - would fail to anxiously search the horizon for potential rescuers? Really?

In fact; the horizon was clear and remained clear and empty until 2nd Officer Boxhall returned to the bridge from the Wireless Room after delivering an amended distress signal.

That was when the first light was seen on the horizon and that was 15 minutes after we stopped and 25 minutes after we hit the iceberg. The ship showing that light was moving toward us. We had no indication from the other ship by wireless so I assumed she was not fitted with the then, fairly new system.

At first we saw her top-most white steaming light, then the second, lower one. At that time detonators for firing the distresss signals were sent for.. Shortly after that we started firing the signals ... not at frequent intervals but at intervals which would guarantee to hold the attention of the approaching ship's crew.

Eventually, I and my officers and some passengers saw he coloured side lights. Then we started calling her up using our powerful Morse signaling light.

She finally stopped for a little while; showed us her white stern light - then she sailed away.

Regardless of the evidence concerning the pretense of that ship, she was virtually ignored by both inquiries. For heaven's sake; why?

That ship was most certainly real and stopped close enough for me to order some of the boats to row over to her, disembarque their passengers, and come back for more.

Perhaps she was ignored because she did not fit-in with the pre-judgements made concerning the movements of the SS Californian? If so- then we have a serious case of manipulation of witness evidence because that vessel could never have been the 'Californian'.

Inaccuracy Number Seven.
The 'Ship's Papers' were not Saved.

It has always been assumed that the official documents, including the Certificate of Registry, Crew and Passenger lists and Official Log Book went down with the ship. However, here is evidence to suggest the contrary.

When I knew the seriousness of the situation, I immediately began developing a plan for abandoning ship.

In every case of abandonment; part of such a plan included saving the 'Ship's Papers'. In fact there was a special bag for storing them in. Unsurprisingly, this was named 'The Ship's Bag'.

Most ships did not have a Purser on board, consequently, the Ship's Bag and Official Papers were kept in the Captain's safe which was usually situated in his cabin.

However; 'Titanic, like all Passenger ships, had Pursers as part of the crew. The Chief Purser's job was much like that of an Hotel Office Manager on shore, in that he and his assistants looked after the day to day paperwork and accounts.

Additionally; he looked after the ships official papers, which; together with the Ship's Bag, he kept in his safe in his office.

When I had developed the basics of my abandonment plan, I called for the Chief Purser to bring the Official Papers and the Ship's Bag to the bridge. Consequently; the man and his assistant arrived beside me shortly after that with the bag which very much resembled a large Gladstone Bag.

I checked the contents - found all in order then added the Scrap Log and engine Movement Book as well as my Night order Book. After that, I gave it back the the Chief Purser and told him to take it along the boat deck and give it to a senior seaman with the instructions it was to be stowed safely in one of the first boats to be launched.

Later, I learned that my orders had been carried out.

Since that time, I have read the transcripts of the Official Inquiries and from them, find that a bag was seen in the hands of a Purser on the starboard side of the boat deck and that an Able Seamen threw a bag into one of the first boats to leave from that side. I also learned from the same source, that a bag was passed-up from a lifeboat to the rescue ship

'Carpathia' and that later; a bag was seen at the Customs & Excise Station in New York.

You might well ask if there is any proof that these documents actually made it to dry-land?

In all honesty; I am unable give you a positive answer to your question. However; one incident which is very well documented might well be all the proof needed.

On Day 2 of the American Official Inquiry, my Third Officer Herbert Pitman was questioned regarding the ship's Log Book. At that time, he denied any knowledge of its fate.

However; two days later, he was questioned again and during that session, was examined regarding the performance of 'Titanic' from the time she left Queenstown in Ireland until the accident.

At that time, he gave some rough figures but could not give exact ones. However the very next day, He provided the US Senate Committee with a memorandum which gave exact days- run figures, clock alterations and average speeds for Noon every day from leaving Queenstown until Noon on April 14, 1912. Where did he get such figures at such short notice? Not from any personal paperwork because he left 'Titanic' empty handed.

Sixteen

Even more Inaccuracies

Inaccuracy Number Eight.
The Lifeboat Plan.

A lay-person could be forgiven for thinking that the lifeboats of 'Titanic' were filled, manned and lowered without a plan or by unskilled individuals. Nothing could be farther from the truth!

Every crew member knew exactly where his or her place was concerning Lifeboat and Fire Drills. Before the ship left home port, each crew member who had a part to play in those drills was allocated a lifeboat and/or Fire Fighting Station.

The Deck Crew were all highly trained, British Government Certificated, Able Seamen and knew exactly what to do in an emergency; many had held similar ranks in the Royal Navy.

These men were organised in two groups termed the Port and Starboard Duty Watches.

On the right, starboard side of the boat deck, the group consisted of Able Seamen commanded by First Officer Murdoch, assisted by Third Officer Pitman and 5th Officer Lowe. They were allocated to boats 1, 3 5, 7, 9, 11 and 15. as well as Collapsible boats 'A' and 'C'.

On the port side of the boat deck, the Able Seamen were commanded by 2nd Officer Lightoller assisted by 4th Officer Boxhall and young 6th Officer Moody. Their boats were evenly numbered; 2, 4, 6, 8, 10, 12, 14 and 16. They too had 2 collapsible boats designates 'B' and 'D'.

Boats 1 and 2 were actually emergency cutters and smaller than the lifeboats. When at sea, these were deployed, one each side and always ready for instant use in case anyone fell over the side. Every evening, the duty Quartermaster would see that a lit oil lamp was placed in each of them and they were only covered when in port.

The collapsible boats were unlike a life boat in that besides being smaller: they did not have rigid wooden sides. In fact, they had canvas sides which - as the name implies - collapsed when the boat was in the stowed position. These were raised and secured before use. They were situated - one each side - on the boat deck inside the emergency cutters. The other two were stowed - one each side of funnel number one. These collapsible boats were launched using the davits previously used for launching the emergency boats after the latter had been sent away.

My Chief Officer Wilde was in overall charge of the operation and had a roving commission. He reported directly to me.

As for me...I wandered about with my megaphone

which I used to send information to boats after they had been launched.

* * *

For a start-off: Since 'Titanic' was sinking by the bow and listed to the starboard (right) side, we had to bring her upright and as level as possible. Thereafter, the plan was to maintain that situation for as long as possible.

To achieve this; lifeboats were filled and lowered progressively - starting from the starboard side forward, these being the heavy' end and the heavy' side.

There was another problem!

As with all passenger ships; 'Titanic' was what is known in the trade as 'Tender'. That means she had a high center of gravity which in turn meant that among other things, she could easily be tilted to one side or the other.

Unfortunately; it did not take much added weight above 'Titanic's' Center of Gravity to make this happen and we were aggravating the situation by adding top weight - by bringing over 2000 people to the upper decks thus locating a mobile weight of as much as 100 tons above the the ship's center of Gravity.

In fact; Chief Officer Wilde demonstrated just how tender she was when, by shifting people from one side to the other side of the boat deck, he was able to level the ship up. However- I diverse!

All the lifeboats were equipped with a set of oars and a

steering oar and the fittings to use them. Each one also had a rudder, sail and mast.

Before embarking occupants, all of these bits of necessary equipment had to be removed and stowed safely to one side on the boat deck. This, after removing the covers and releasing the restrains, was the second chore for the sailors. After that, the boats were then lowered to the embarkation position. Only then, were they ready to receive occupants.

On 'Titanic' there were three embarkation positions. The first was directly from the boat deck. The second was from the deck below - Deck 'A'. However the latter was enclosed by windows at its forward end therefore these had to be opened beforehand.

However, the main means of embarkation for fit and able people was via the gangway doors on the lower decks, using Jacob's ladders provided at every boat.

Each boat was suspended from the launching davit by two 2.5 inch diameter manila ropes - one at each end. The boat was lowered by slacking these ropes evenly and simultaneously around two deck-mounted bollards. The terms 'evenly' and 'simultaneously' are most important when considering the weight of the load and this is where, yet another bit of misunderstanding arises. I mean the number of people loaded into each lifeboat

<u>Inaccuracy Number Nine</u>
<u>The Lifeboat Filling Procedures.</u>

I have seen and read numerous sources which declare that the Lifeboats of 'Titanic' were improperly loaded and that if they had been fully loaded before lowering, many more would have been saved. This is true in theory, but was totally impracticable for several reasons.

As I explained; the boats were lowered by slacking a rope at each end and that such slacking had to be done smoothly and equally. In this way, the boat remained level and the weight of it and its contents were evenly shared between two single lowering ropes.

However; if one rope was slackened at a different rate from the other, the boat hung unevenly. This was a moment of great danger.

Normally, during the lowering operation, a man was located at each end of the boat to slacken a rope called a 'fall' and an officer was stationed between these two to oversee the smoothness of the operation.

If, during the lowering process, one rope was slackened-off faster than the other, the officer would order the man on the longer rope to 'hold-on'! In other words...stop slacking-off his rope!

However; if this order was carried out abruptly, a sudden shock load would be introduced into the 'held-on' rope and if that shock load was greater than the strength of the rope, the rope in question would suddenly break.

When such a thing happens, the boat swings vertically - spilling the contents. Then the remaining rope also breaks due to overloading. In a word - disaster!

Consequently; a trained seaman will avoid a situation where such a situation can occur. In 'Titanic'; this was easier said than done.

On land; an example of this would be when towing

another motor car. If the driver of the vehicle being towed stamps on the brake, the tow-rope will break.

However; let's consider the practice of the day back in 1912, concerning filling and lowering ship's lifeboats

'Titanic' was equipped with the very latest lifeboat launching davits. These were a vast improvement on the ones normally in use at that time. Most ships a that time used the old, Radial type davits and the standard practice with them was to lower the boat empty, then fill it from the deck using the an embarkation ladder called a 'Jacob's Ladder'.

This was a long, portable rope ladder fitted with rungs made of flat wooden steps. The Regulations stated that one such ladder should be allocated to each lifeboat and each ladder should be long enough to be able to reach the sea at the ship's lightest draft. In most ships, such ladders were rolled-up and stored beside, under or within each lifeboat. As I pointed out earlier; there was one of these for each boat on 'Titanic'.

As for the process of loading itself? I can very well understand the modern-day outrage expressed regarding the way we loaded our lifeboats on 'Titanic' that dreadful morning, but such outrage is based on a lack of understanding of the attitudes of the day.

As I explained earlier - we had to consider the strength of the rope materials and method of boat-lowering, but we were also confronted with another two problem which seems to have escaped the consideration of those people nowadays who criticise our method of loading the boats.

These problems, were the physical strength of women and children and the way women dressed back in 1912. Long flowing dresses were not compatible with clambering down the side of a ship by way of a Jacob's Ladder. Nor were such means of access designed for use by babies and small children.

Many prefer to believe that the romantic 'women first' order was given as an act of chivalry; In fact, no such order was given by me or any of my officers.

The women and children action arose from the panic of a particular passenger and that passenger was our Company Chairman...Joseph Ismay.

Early-on, I had the negative report from my Carpenter regarding the extent and rate of flooding. However; I did not immediately accept it, but verified it by brief, personal inspection. That was when the order for all hands on deck was made.

Around that time; Chairman Ismay arrived on the bridge wearing a dressing gown and slippers and asking what was happening. I very foolishly told him of my concerns and added that I did not think that at the then rate of flooding, we would last very long. He went away and I thought no more of it... I had a lot on my mind and was otherwise engaged.

After the men had mustered on the boat deck and the lifeboats had almost been made ready; I was on the port side of the bridge when Third Officer Pitman arrived by my side He seemed embarrassed and very agitated and blurted-out -

"Sorry to bother you sir at this time, but there is a passenger down at boat number five causing a panic."

I calmed the lad down then made him explain.

Young Pitman told me that there was a man dressed in slippers and dressing gown at boat number five who he thought might be our Chairman and that the man was telling everyone that we had no time to loose and urging me to immediately begin embarking the women and children.

I asked him if there were any women and children in the vicinity to which he replied in the affirmative. Then I thought for another moment and concluded that this might be a good idea.

As I said; normal practice when launching and filling a lifeboat was to fist put on board a boat crew - lower the boat to the water - then embark passengers using a Jacob's Ladder. However, as I also pointed out; these ladies were in no way properly attired to use a boarding ladder.

In addition, ladies and children were much lighter than their male counterparts. Consequently; I told Pitman to carry on and humour the man.

There is a modern concept that since the HMS Birkenhead affair sixty years before 'Titanic'... the unwritten rule at sea concerning the loading of lifeboats, has been 'women and children first'. In fact that was and still is a Victorian land person's romantic interpretation and most certainly not a rule - written or otherwise. However, I must admit it sounds profoundly noble and chivalrous to the modern mind... particularly when the truth is that the present-day attitude seems to be 'every person for themselves'.

Inaccuracy Number Ten.
Preferential treatment allocating lifeboat Places.

It is inferred and sometimes declared as fact, that preferential treatment was given according to rank and wealth. That is grossly untrue, and for one simple reason.

To be able to allocate lifeboats in such a way, those doing the allocating must be able to instantly recognise individuals in a poorly lit area. On 'Titanic' this was patently not the case.

To begin with - only Deck Officers had the power to allocate a boat place and out of the six such officers on 'Titanic' only me...the captain...was in daily contact with passengers and knew the important ones. The Deck officers had no contact with passengers and ate in their own mess-room up on the boat deck. As a matter of fact - the crew had been together for such a brief time before the disaster, that most of them did not know some of their fellow shipmates or officers much less important personages.

This accusation arises from the fact that a dignitary such as Sir Cosmo Duff-Gordon and his wife as well at Chairman Ismay were allowed to board a boat when so many were lost.

One fact regarding this has been completely ignored, and that is the attitude of 'Titanic' as she was sinking.

As she sank, the ship was down by the bow, thus creating an upward-sloping deck - sloping upward toward the stern and away from danger... the sea. For this reason many people moved away from that danger and walked up the sloping decks toward the stern and away from where the lifeboats were. Several crew members were included among them. The result of this, combined with fear of the unknown by some passengers, resulted in a shortage of those gathering on the boat deck beside the boats. So much so, that near the end, those loading the boats were finding that 'customers' were becoming scarce.

Along with a few other male passengers and crew members, our Chairman Ismay spent the entire time on the boat deck moving from boat to boat and helping where ever he could. During that time, Sir Cosmo and Lady Duff-Gordon stood aside not attempting to board any boat. It was only at the very end, when there were no other people on the boat deck that these three were ordered into a boat and it was not a lifeboat but the rescue cutter number 1 - the last proper boat to leave that side. Even then, Ismay only left because he was physically forced to and assumed, that since there were only a few of us left - those remaining after he had gone would board the last collapsible boat after the cutter had gone.

I see it's getting late, so I suggest we finish-up for the day. Please take these notes back to your hotel and study them carefully over the next few days. You will see that they begin at the very beginning and deal with these inaccuracies in a chronological manner. After you have done so, we can resume the interview back here. I am in no hurry. However; I'm sure that after you have read these observations you will have more questions to ask. Oh! and by the way- when going through these, I suggests you have beside you, a copy of the transcripts of the evidence given by survivors at both Official Inquiries. They are readily available on the Internet

Seventeen

ANOTHER QUESTION

Good morning, everyone! I trust you all had a restful couple of days away from having your ears tortured by my ravings?

You did? I am pleased to hear it!. I will make tea and coffee for us all then we can settle down and continue with my story.

Well! now that the inner-selves have been fortified - shall we continue? Do you have any more questions after reading my notes on inconsistencies?

"It's great to see you again, captain. We did as you suggested and searched through your written notes on inaccuracies with a fine tooth-comb. I must say; you were extremely thorough in your analysis and might add… patient…with our lack of marine understanding.

We all agree that the 'Titanic' tragedy will engage historians for years to come, but your observations have enlightened us more than we could ever have imagined.

However, we do not. at this time, have more than one question which we would like to hear your opinion on.

In your notes, you briefly mentioned the part played in the disaster by the captain and officers of the Leyland Line vessel named SS Californian.

As you are probably very well aware - these men did not come out of the affair shiny, clean and smelling of roses. In fact; it seems to officialdom and the general public that they acted as cowards. What are your thoughts on that matter?"

Well, as you are now aware; I had no knowledge if the SS Californian at the time 'Titanic' sank. It was only many years later when I returned to civilisation and was able to see the moving pictures in which she was mentioned that I learned of her existence. Finally, when I was able to get my hands on copies of the transcripts of the proceedings of both the Official Inquiries, I was able to form opinions regarding that vessel, her crew and Captain. At the same time; I learned she was the second vessel I had seen in the vicinity of the wreck site that dreadful morning of April 15, 1912. When I *did* eventually read about how her captain and crew were treated by Officialdom, the press and the general public, I was filled with disgust and disbelief that honourable men would act in such a way. In fact; had you not asked me about it; I had made my mind up that after contacting you, I was going to do my damndness to expose the outrageous nonsense that was written then and is perpetuated to this day about the men of the 'Californian, but since you asked...

Eighteen

THE SS CALIFORNIAN

As I mentioned earlier; ever since I was able to research the full story concerning the 'Californinan', I have been filled with amazement, disgust and anger in equal portions.

Never, in my entire life, have I seen a more blatant, outrageous travesty of justice so publicly broadcast and accepted by not only the general public, who have at least an excuse for doing so, but by Officialdom - those purporting to be versed in the interpretation of marine matters.

Allow me to go over it in detail. I again apologise in advance if I wander too deep into technicalities.

Where possible, I'll try and avoid any confusion and if necessary; draw you a little sketch to clarify my point.

Let me begin with the current ideas on the matter.

As we all know; both the US and UK Official Inquiries reached much the same conclusion regarding the actions of the captain and officers of the SS Californian during the 'Titanic' disaster, but were they correct?

Let's start with what the Americans said about her captain - Captain Stanley Lord. I'll use a quote from the official deliberations made by the US Senate Sub-committee at the end of their Official Inquiry.

'The committee is forced to the inevitable conclusion that the Californian, controlled by the same company, was nearer the Titanic than the 19 miles reported by her captain, and that her officers and crew saw the distress signals of the Titanic and failed to respond to them in accordance with the dictates of humanity, international usage, and the requirements of law. The only reply to the distress signals was a counter signal from a large white light which was flashed for nearly two hours from the mast of the Californian. In our opinion such conduct, whether arising from indifference or gross carelessness, is most reprehensible, and places upon the commander the Californian a grave responsibility.'

In his summing-up of the case, The British Commissioner of Wrecks..Lord Mersey compounded the felony by writing:

"These circumstances convince me that the ship seen by the "Californian" was the "Titanic," and if so, according to Captain Lord, the two vessels were about five miles apart at the time of the disaster. The evidence from the "Titanic" corroborates this estimate, but I am advised that the distance was probably greater, though not more than eight to ten miles.

Utter nonsense! What *'forced'* the Americans to come to such a conclusion?

What *'convinced'* Lord Mersey to write what he wrote?

Were the interrogators of the 'Californian's' captain and officers on both sides of the Atlantic asleep when these witnesses were giving evidence? Or were their technical Marine Advisers off on vacation at the time?

I ask these questions because anyone who passed the 7th Grade in school and who has learned to read and understand the English language (and who had read the sworn evidence by witnesses) could be forgiven for thinking so. How on earth could these 'learned' individuals have arrived at such conclusions?

The author of that final US report - Senator William Alden Smith and most of the members of his Senate Sub-committee were present throughout the question of the captain and crew of the 'Clifornian' and had afterward, read the transcript of the evidence given by them. That being the case; they could not have missed the sworn evidence which told them that these officers most certainly did see pyrotechnic signals and that said signals did not rise very high above the horizon. Nor did these signals rise very high above the deck-level of a ship which had stopped nearby.

However, and more to the point...these Senate Sub-committee members were advised by skilled experts from the US Navy - skilled officers who knew perfectly well that any trained sailor seeing such a sight, could not have mistaken it for the universally recognised description of distress signals at sea.

The same applies to Lord Mersey who also had eminent marine scholars to assist him in his deliberations.

I pause at this point, because that is the time when the interrogations themselves should also have been paused and the presence of the vessel which had stopped nearby, ignored.

I say this because that nearby vessel was a 'red herring' which diverted the attention of the interrogators from the true situation.

If that vessel had not been there; there would have been no reason for Inquiry officials to attempt to make a direct connection between her and the sinking 'Titanic'. However, no one denies that the signals *were* seen by those on 'Californian' and that these signals *were* from 'Titanic'.

So let's go back to the evidence of the accused given at the Official Inquiries and learn what really happened.

On being told of the sighting of a single pyrotechnic signal which had no formal identity; Captain Lord of the 'Californian' did as I, or any other captain, would have done - he ordered his men to get as much information as they could, then report back to him. We know they obeyed that order.

Before continuing, I remind you of the circumstances of the case at that time which were:

(1) Only one vessel in the vicinity had been heard using wireless before the nearby vessel stopped and that was the 'Titanic'. Therefore it is unlikely that the unknown vessel had wireless.

(2) Frequent, unsuccessful attempts to contact the nearby vessel using a powerful signaling light had been made by 'Californian's' officers since that vessel had stopped.

(3) There was no sense of urgency to the situation. The signals being seen *did not convey* urgency.

(4) The signals seen did not conform to any internationally recognised protocol. They were simply rocket-type signals seen at irregular intervals in the direction of, but not necessarily from, the nearby, stopped ship.

(5) The nearby ship had been stopped for over an hour without any attempt to make contact with 'Californian' or acknowledge that she was even there.

(6) These signals were described as 'appearing to come from beyond' that nearby ship. In other words 'far-off - in the distance'. Anyone who has actually seen such a thing will immediately recognise the description.

Oh! and here is yet another glaring inconsistency.

The the nearby vessel seen by Captain Lord had been seen approaching from the eastward about 10-55pm and stopped around 11-30 pm 'Californian' ship time. However, that was not the only vessel that stopped within sight of the 'Californian' around that time.

At the British Inquiry held in London, 3rd Officer Groves of the SS Californian told his questioners that from about 11-10 pm until 11-40pm., he watched a vessel approaching the stopped 'Californian' from the southward not from the eastward. Consequently; his was the description of a vessel approaching 'Californian' from an entirely different direction than the one seen by his captain. Not only that, but he saw it 15 minutes later and stopping 10 minutes after the one seen by Captain Lord.

At this point; you should know that ship times on that night, differed from ship to ship. I appreciate this may cause some confusion, therefore, to simplify matters; I will continue from here-on by reducing all ship times to the common denominator of Greenwich Mean Time - GMT. I'll do this by applying the difference between ship time and GMT to each ship time. I will conclude with a table of events and times so that you can plainly see the relevance of the arguments.

Now let's continue by looking at this from the 'other side of the fence' so to speak - from the point of view of the 'Titanic' survivors.

According to 'Titanic' witnesses James Collins and Patrick Dillon; 'Titanic' hit the iceberg at 0300am GMT and her engines finally stopped six minutes later, at 03-06am GMT. Their evidence is confirmed by the evidence given by Titanic's 2nd Officer Lightoller who told his questioners that he was on deck 3 minutes after 'Titanic' hit the ice berg and at that time the vessel was slowing down and making about 6 knots.

The foregoing plainly shows that if 'Titanic' stopped at 03-06am GMT the vessels seen by Captain Lord and his 3rd Officer could not have been the 'Titanic', since she stopped 26 minutes *after* 2-20am GMT; the time that the vessel seen by Captain Lord had stopped and 16 minutes after the one seen by 3rd Officer Groves had stopped..

The evidence also tells us that 3rd officer Groves of the 'Californian' watched a vessel approaching the 'Californian' for thirty minutes.

Again; when we measure that against the evidence of the survivors; that vessel could never have been 'Titanic'.

To top it all... I know for absolute certain, that there were no vessels around when 'Titanic' did stop and if you don't believe me... read the evidence given by the surviving lookouts who were specifically asked about that.

So how many miles really separated these three stopped vessels which must have been in sight of each other? By which I mean (1) 'Californian', (2) Captain Lord's mystery vessel and (3) the mystery vessel seen by 3rd officer Groves? Let's look at the evidence again -this time; in greater detail.

Captain Lord said, his mystery vessel stopped four (4) miles away; how did he know that?

Lord had a clear view of the horizon through his binoculars. He would have seen the nearby ship's lights relative to the horizon. Knowing that his visible horizon was 8 miles away, he would have been able to make a fairly accurate estimate of the separation distance 'Californian' to ship and ship to horizon.

Likewise; Groves said *his* vessel stopped 6 miles away to the south. However, Captain Lord said there was pack ice half a mile to the south and the ice itself was about 1 to 3 miles wide. This being so, then that vessel had to have been on the far side of the ice.

Here's is another important indicator:

3rd officer Groves of 'Californian' said he had first seen his mystery vessel when 12 miles away. If so, and that vessel stopped six miles from 'Californian' after steaming for half an hour from the time of first sighting; then *his* vessel was only making 12 knots whereas, 'Titanic' was making 22.5 knots!

This also means that since the vessel Groves saw had been steaming on a northerly course for 30 minutes she could not have been 'Titanic' because as I told you and as the evidence proves; 'Titanic' only ran for 6 minutes after hitting the iceberg.

Earlier, I stated that there was no doubt that the signals seen on 'Californian' most certainly came from 'Titanic'. How can I be so sure?

Quartermaster George Rowe - the man who fired the first signal on 'Titanic'- stated that he did so at 04-07 GMT. But what was the equivalent ship time on the 'Californian?

In his evidence to the Inquiry, 'Californian's' Second Officer Herbert Stone told his questioner that he had seen a flash in the sky in the direction of the nearby vessel at around 4-05am GMT that morning which he thought was a shooting star but a few minutes later, he saw as second light in the sky which he identified as a rocket.

If that rocket was the one fired by Rowe from 'Titanic' then the time was 04-07am GMT. This suggests that Captain Lord had altered his clocks by 10 minutes to match the position where he had stopped. This to any Navigator would be a reasonable caution since Lord did not know how long he would be stopped there. It also means that 'a few minutes after' would have been a few minutes after 04-05am GMT which matches the time of firing the first signal given by QM Rowe of 'Titanic'.

The foregoing proves beyond all reasonable doubt that the rockets seen from 'Californian' were indeed, fired from the sinking 'Titanic'. However, it also proves that not one, but two unidentified vessels stopped in sight of the stopped 'Californian' and - that neither of them was the 'Titanic' and additionally; that both of them eventually left the scene before daylight.

The foregoing should be enough to convince all but the most sceptical of individuals. However for such people, there is yet more incontrovertible proof that 'Californian' and 'Titanic' were never in sight of each other. This proof can be found in the evidence given by 'Californian's 2nd

Officer Herbert Stone and her only Navigation Apprentice, James Gibson.

At the UK Inquiry, both these young men swore that they saw the bursting flash of rocket signal way down on the south eastern horizon. The ship time was around 03-20 am (6-40am GMT) - forty minutes before the end of their Watch duty. At that time, 'Californian' was still stopped and the sea was clear of all other vessels.

Now this is very important, because if any lights, be it rockets or otherwise, are seen right on the horizon, they are being seen at their maximum range and also at the maximum range of the observer. This means that if we know the height of a rocket above the sea and the height of eye of the observer seeing it above the sea, then, we can calculated the exact distance between the observer and source of the rocket.

We know the height of eye of those on the 'Californian' upper bridge was about 55 feet which means the visible horizon was 8.8 miles away.

We also know from the evidence given at the inquiries by Captain Rostron of the 'Carpathia' that at that time, he was firing signal rockets of comfort to assure the survivors of 'Titanic he was on the way'.

It follows that the rockets seen right on the horizon by the 'Californian's men were the ones fired by Captain Rostron. However; this is not the only information we have.

Captain Rostron said he arrive at the survivors at 4 am.(7-14am GMT). That being so, and the fact that his ship was making 14.5 knots, tells us that at the time Stone and Gibson saw his rockets, 'Carpathia' was around 10 miles from the 'Titanic' survivors in boats. Since we also know the course she was steering (303T), we can easily plot the position of 'Carpathia' when he fired those rockets'

I won't bore you all with the mathematics...as they say: 'here's a little sketch I prepared earlier'. I apologise for the poor quality of the sketch. As you can all see, it's not to scale and drawing was never one of my strong-points. However I'm sure that it is clear enough to satisfy everyone except members of the 'Flat Earth Society.

Incidentally: I notice elsewhere that later thinking, places the separation distance between the sinking 'Titanic' and the stopped SS Californian to be 19.1 miles. However the authors of this continue to perpetuate the claim that the vessels were in sight of each other from beginning to end. As the evidence shows - that claim is absurd.

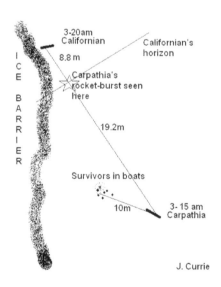

As a matter of coincidence.. that distance of 19.1 nautical miles was the one claimed by Captain Lord - the distance between the Stopped 'Californian' and the incorrect distress position worked by Joe Boxhall - the one all potential rescue vessels, including the 'Californian', headed for. It is also a mile longer that the initial separation distance suggested by the evidence of 'Californian's' 3rd Officer Groves! Food for thought?

I hope you have been able to follow the foregoing explanations and that now. you can see that there is no doubt that the sinking 'Titanic' and the stopped 'Californian' were never in sight of each other. Not only that, but that the Authorities on both sides of the Atlantic were complacent in the blatantly dishonest findings against the officer of the 'Californian'.

In fact; as it see it- the descendants of these poor lads who went to their graves despised as irresponsible incompetent cowards by the world have a very strong case of libel against both the US and UK Governments of the day.

I appreciate that the foregoing may be a little too much to swallow in a single reading, so as promised earlier here is a table of times and events. Close comparison between these times will prove my point.

I remind you that all reported ship times have been reduced to the common denominator of GMT.

Event	GMT
'Californian' stops.	01-31am.
Lord's mystery ship stops	02-40am.
Groves' mystery ship stops.	02-50am.
'Titanic' stops.	03-06am.
'Titanic fires first signal.	04-07am.
2/0/Stone sees first signal.	04-07am.
'Titanic' fires last signal.	04-47am.
'Titanic' sinks.	05-25am.

The popular belief is that we were afloat for 2 hours 36 minutes after we stopped but as you can see; we were only afloat for a mere 2 hours and 25 minutes.

Nineteen

ANOTHER QUESTION

"Thank you Captain. So it is clear that these men on 'Californian' went to their graves wrongfully condemned.

We were wondering: Obviously you do not have first-hand information concerning the events following the sinking. However, as you say; you have have carefully read all the available evidence given to both Official Inquiries by the survivors of the disaster and have admirably demonstrated your findings regarding the part played by the SS Californian. Have you any other observations regarding any of the other major players in the drama?"

In fact, while you were away, I did spend a lot of time going over that very subject. Yes; I do have other observations to make... in particular regarding the conduct of my Fourth Officer Joseph Boxhall and that of the accepted 'hero' of the event ...Henry Rostron; captain of the RMS Carpathia.

I will start with young Joe Boxhall.

117

Twenty

JOSEPH BOXHALL

I had sailed with young Boxhall before 'Titanic' and knew him to be a well-qualified and experienced young Deck Officer.

Like many of my officers; Boxhall had two Master's Certificates. He was a fully certified Master Mariner in Sail, and had also passed the extra qualification of Master Mariner -Steam.

Up to, including and after the moment we hit the iceberg, Boxhall acted with the utmost efficiency. He was a first class Navigator and it was he who completed the lengthy calculations of the six sextant observations taken earlier that evening by Second Officer Lightoller. In fact; of these six - Boxhall calculated five of them. 3rd Officer Pitman calculated the first one and handed the rest to Boxhall when the latter relieved him on Watch at 8pm.

I remember Boxhall coming to me sometime after 9 pm that evening; proudly announcing that he had completed the calculations and that they located the 'Titanic' right where she should have been... on her pre-determined track for New York.

Boxhall worked with Young Moody... the Sixth Officer and youngest member of my bridge team. At the moment we hit the ice berg, he was in his cabin having a cup of tea. I was next door in my cabin, resting on the couch.

As was my usual practice... I intended to visit the bridge when 3rd Officer Pitman took over from Boxhall, which was the end of Log Book April 14 and make sure the planned clock change had been completed before turning-in for the night.

It was getting close to Midnight when the first clock change was due to be made, Boxhall finished his tea and headed for the Chart Room; he wanted to make sure Moody had performed the task of applying the first half of that planned clock alteration.

He had only covered half the distance to the fore-bridge when all hell let loose. Murdoch shouted his helm order... ran the the engine telegraph and she hit. That was the beginning of the end of 'Titanic'.

Boxhall arrived in the covered-in bridge area at the same time as I did and the Stand-by Quartermaster was right there with us. The rest you know about!

However; Boxhall did not simply stand around like a knot in a thread waiting for orders - Oh no! - He immediately headed off down below to the lower forward decks to have a look-see for himself. I had looked for him, intending to tell him to do so but he had already acted.

In less than ten minutes, he was back on the bridge with a favourable report. Bless his innocence! As we know that turned sour very quickly. However this was an example of the man himself - a man who acted on his own initiative. It was that very same initiative that made him, as far as I am concerned, the true hero of the 'Titanic' disaster... and here's why.

You will recall I told you that when I ordered Boxhall into safety boat 2, he ran back into the wheelhouse and collected a box of Company green-colored signal flares? Well! had it not been for these flares, I might not be here giving this interview and more to the point - the body count for the disaster might have been very much higher. Because the firing off of one of those green flares in answer to one the 'comfort' rockets sent up by Rostron on the 'Carpathia' was the only reason that the survivors were found. Had Boxhall not fired that green flare - 'Carpathia' would have passed to the northward of Boxhall in Boat 2 and possibly run into the pack ice herself. Imagine it!

OK! I here your counter-remarks concerning Boxhall's mistake when calculating the the distress position everyone headed for... but stop and think about that.

When Boxhall asked me if he would send a corrected distress position; he made his way into the Chart Room where - to calculate the distress position - he used the ship's true position calculated earlier that evening and a course and speed from there to where we stopped after hitting the ice berg.
So how did he get it so wrong?

Two things:

(1) He assumed a speed o 22 knots instead of using the 22.5 knot speed indicated by the Patent log and...

(2) He assumed that the time of stopping recorded in the Scrap Log was a time which included the full amount of the planned 47 minute clock set- back.

Boxhall simply made the twin mistakes of assuming speed and lapsed time. In fact, had he used the correct lapsed time and speed, these would have given him the proper distance run from the evening position and brought potential rescuers to the correct distress position.

This begs the question: Where would that have put the RMS Carpathia?

Goodness me! is that the time? Sorry folks I got carried away and forgot that you all have a journey to make. I'll stop now and let you get back to your hotel. See you all tomorrow; have an enjoyable evening. Good night!

Twenty One

R.M.S. CARPATHIA

Good morning my friends! I trust you are rested well.

By now you must be getting tired of listening to my haverings and seeing my wrinkled, old features. Never mind - it won't be long now. If all goes well; I suspect I'll get to the end of the story some time today.

Yesterday, I told you why I thought that young Joe Boxhall was, as far as I am concerned, the true hero of the 'Titanic' disaster. Today, I'm going to suggest - horror of horrors - that Captain Rostron and his RMS Carpathia crew were anything but heroes. To do so, I will relate the story as derived from the evidence given by Rostron himself at both Official Inquiries.

During the late evening of April 14, 1912, 'Carpathia' was following an easterly track which was about 35 miles south of the westerly track being followed by 'Titanic'. She was four days out from New York and bound for several Mediterranean ports via Gibraltar. Like the 'Californian', she had a single Marconi Wireless operator; a man by the name of Harold Cottam.

Cottam's evidence to the Inquiries was vague and imprecise. Essentially; he told his questioners that just before midnight on April 14, he was thinking of going to bed and while doing so, listening to the news being transmitted from the Marconi Station at Cape Cod, USA.

At the end of these bulletins, Cape Cod usually sent messages for ships with two Operators, but Cottam decided to listen-in.

During the transmission, he heard several messages for 'Titanic' so he copied them down with the intention of passing them on to us the following morning. Now, why he would do such a thing I have no idea. He knew we had two Operators and our Wireless Station was continuously manned. Even stranger; he then said he called us up to tell us about these messages and that was when he discovered that we were in trouble and wrote down our distress position. It was the amended one worked-out by Joe Boxhall.

This begs the question - if he could hear us then why didn't he hear our earlier distress calls giving our original distress position - the one I worked out earlier?

Even more strange: when that young man was questioned later in London, he told the Inquiry that he did not keep a record of his communications with 'Titanic' because he was 'too busy'.

Too busy doing what? His only task was to communicate and keep records of his communications.

During my research, I have discovered that there was

one ship equipped with wireless which passed within sight of 'Titanic's iceberg four hours before we hit it, but did not send out a warning. The message appeared in a wireless message filed with the US Hydrogaphic Office when the vessel in question docked in the US. That vessel was the SS Parisian and her filed message reads:

'April 14, 4:30 P.M., latitude 41 55' N., longitude 49 02' W., passed first iceberg. 8 P.M., latitude 41 42' N., longitude 49 55' W., passed last iceberg. Between positions passed 14 medium and large icebergs and numerous growlers.'

The last iceberg position in the above message is 2 miles southward of where the wreck of the 'Titanic now lies. However; note the time of when that last berg was seen-8pm - four hours *before* we hit it!

Additionally - at 8 pm that evening, 'Carpathia' would have been little more than 25 miles south of the 'Parisian'.

There is something not quite right here! 'Carpathia's wireless Operator Cottam said that before he heard of our plight, he had been in contact with the 'Parisian' and was waiting for a reply. The two vessels must have been very close at the time and 'Parisian' was sill in the process of skirting the ice area; yet not a word is said about ice. In fact Captain Rostron very clearly stated the the first he heard about ice was when he received our distress call.

Something distinctly smells of 'Italian cheese' - don't you think? That same lad Cottam was told by Marconi himself to 'keep his mouth shut' before they met in Marconi's New York hotel when 'Carpathia' arrived at New York.

The foregoing is not the only strange parts of the

'Carpathia' story. Her captain - Captain Rostron made some very strange remarks during the time *he* was interrogated. I suspect that these were whitewashed-over and ignored to maintain his image as the hero of the day. But was he in truth - a hero? let's find out.

As I said earlier; 'Carpathia' was to the south of the sinking 'Titanic' and heading in the opposite direction.

Due to the prevarications of her wireless operator, we cannot be sure exactly when her captain received our distress call, but from subsequent evidence we do know where she was when she did receive it.

In fact, like his Wireless Operator Cottam - Captain Rostron did not seem very sure of events around that time. His Public Inquiry version in the UK differed substantially from the version he first gave in the US.

In the US, Rostron told his questioners that he was in bed when made aware of 'Titanic's plight - that his Watch-keeping bridge officers burst into his room and gave him the news.

On the other hand - in the UK, he said that it was his Wireless Operator, Cottam who burst into his room and gave him the news.

Then we have his contradictory tales about his speed and when he arrived on the scene.

According to Captain Rostron; 'Carpathia' was 58 miles to the southeastward of 'Titanic' when he received the distress signal and he turned his ship and pointed her directly at the position given. However; you must all remember that this was not the true position but in fact, was the incorrect one worked by Joe Boxwall. Consequently; 'Carpathia' was pointing in the wrong direction from the very moment Rostron turned her around. Despite this - 'Carpathia' arrived at the true site of the disaster So how on earth did that come about? Think about it!

Rostron also told us he would be at the distress position in 4 hours, then he changed it to 4-30 am. That' fits perfectly since 'Carpathia' was 14 knot ship and 58 divided by 14.5... the speed Rostron exected her to make....equals 4. However; he had to change his speed story when, due to sighting Boxhall's green flares, he in fact arrived half an hour early, at 4 am. As a cover-up, he simply dividing the total distance of 58 miles to the wrong position by 3.5 instead of 4 and concocting a ridiculous story to the effect that he put on extra boiler room staff and increased his old ship's speed to 16.6 knots.

The foregoing could be excused except for the fact that Rostron must have known his mistake very soon after rescuing the survivors. Because at 9 am that morning he took his ship southward before heading west toward his destination of New York. Three hours later, at Noon on April 15, he knew exactly where his ship was relative to the position he had recently left -the true distress position. Consequently he and his officers must have realised that they were farther east than first thought and consequently the original distress position was wrong.

Yet that valiant man Rostron, assured poor Joe Boxhall and everyone else that Boxhall's distress position was 'excellent'. In fact.. I later discovered that Joe believed him to the point whereby when he, Boxhall, died many years later, he had his ashes scattered over the incorrect distress position.

Whatever way we wish to look at it - the captain and officers of the RMS Carpathia were incompetent Navigators to say the least and it was by pure luck... not by skilled seamanship, that they found themselves praised to high heaven.

I cannot believe that professionals back then did not see these gaping faults that I have just shown to you, but the end result - the rescue of the survivors - excited the press and the public, so I guess they simply buried what I have just shown you.

Twenty Two

WIRELESS RECORDS

I almost forgot to tell you about the problem with the recording of wireless messages and the strange, conflicting information given at both Official Inquiries by the employees of the Marconi Company.

Recently, when I read the evidence given by the Wireless Operator on the RMS Carpathia - what I read caused me to look into the stories in more detail. I therefore delved deeper into the sworn statements given by my own Junior Operator, Bride and the statements given by employees serving on the vessels 'Carpathia' and 'Mount Temple'.

You will remember that I told you that Cottam, who was the operator on 'Carpathia', did not keep a Wireless Log list of the exchanges between his ship and us from before he accidentally heard our cry for help, until after it was all over - giving the reason for not doing so to be that he was too busy. Heavens! the man was a Wireless Operator - he had nothing else to do but send and receive wireless messages. I do not accept that excuse, nor should have any responsible individual. However, we do have the wireless Log (Process-verbal) kept by....., the Opertor on the 'Mount Temple'. Her Captain produced it as evidence at the US Inquiry.

Durrant, who was the Marconi Operator on 'Mount Temple' *did* receive the first distress signal - the one I calculated, but strangely enough; he did not record it in his log book nor did he mention it when questioned in London.

According to the evidence; he simply wrote it on a scrap of paper and delivered it to his captain. Fortunately, Captain Moore kept it in his pocket and produced it as evidence at the American Inquiry who put it on record. Otherwise; the world would never have heard about it.

So why did Durrant fail to mention the first distress signal - even although we know he received it?-. Now that too is strange. Here's yet another inconsistency.

In his evidence to the British Inquiry, Durrant said that at night, his apparatus could reach a distance of 200 nautical miles. Yet; in his official record he had recorded the following;

"9452. Just read your account, as you have it there [In a copy of his Wireless Log] - *"Titanic" sending C.Q.D. Answer him, but he says, "Cannot read you, old man. Here my position, 41° 46' N. 50° 14' W. Come at once, have struck berg." I advised my captain.*

At a distance of 60 miles, Durrant's signals would have been blasting off the ears of our Operators! In fact; the UK questioners noticed this inconsistency and grilled him about it

There are so many irregularities and inaccurate notations in the 'Mount Temple' Process-Verbal Wireless Log submitted in the USA. I will deal with them one by one. Keep in mind that the times given are New York Eastern Standard time.

(1) The time recorded for 'Mount Temple' receiving the amended distress position is 10-25 pm yet the time recorded for her turning toward 'Titanic' is 15 minutes later - at 10-40 pm. This does not fit with the evidence given by her captain to the effect that he turned immediately after he received the first distress position and then adjusted his course when he received the amended position at 10-25pm

(2) Despite the fact that the SS Frankfurt was the first vessel to respond to our original distress call - she is not mentioned as responding until 10-48 pm - 23 minutes after the amended distress call was transmitted.

(3) Despite the claims by 'Carpathia's Operator that he was too busy o keep a record.... the record of the 'Mount Temple shows that 'Carpathia' was only in contact with Titanic once after her accidental receipt of our amended distress position.

(4) The record hows us telling the RMS Olympic that we were sinking and to have her boats ready. Why on earth would we say such a thing when we knew we had less than two hours to live and that she would not be in our vicinity for another sixteen hours?

Pardon the pun but the foregoing was only the tip of the 'Marconi' ice berg, I suspect that our Italian genius was very active behind the scene. I sighted a telegram from him to the 'Carpathia' operator, sent as 'Carpathia' was heading up channel toward her berth at new York. it was an order for Cottam to attend his boss at the latter's new York Hotel and contained the following words 'Keep your mouth shut until you get here'.

Twenty Three

ANY FINAL QUESTIONS?

Well gentlemen! - I cannot think of any more 'Titanic' stories at present which might interest you or your audiences. if you, in turn have no questions for me, I think we'll have a cup of tea and bring this interview to a close. No doubt I'll think of something the moment your vehicles disappear from sight. Perhaps one of you will do the same. If so, you all know where to find me. At my age, I don't think I'll be doing any more traveling.

I must say: I'm very glad you accepted my invitations to come and listen to me and to have met you all. I have enjoyed our daily sessions immensely.

I don't know what you will do with all that I have told you, but no doubt you will inform me eventually

We certainly have covered a fair mileage of information concerning my old ship 'Titanic'. I am just sad that I didn't get from her that wonderful experience a captain gets when sailing his new ship into New York for the very first time.

I have to confess that after many years catching up

with this world of ours, and digesting the mountains of media concerning the loss of the 'Titanic' and reading the fanciful rubbish printed about her - I was fairly bursting to tell you what really happened but now that I have got it off my chest... I don't know what I feel. Certainly not relief or anything like that.

I suppose if I really think about it - my first sincere wish is that the world would stop treating that horrible disaster like a money-making circus. That people would treat the dead as all civilised folk should treat them and stop to think how they, as individuals, would like to be treated by those remaing after *they* have passed to that vast ocean in the sky.

In mentioning the dead; I hope that those in authority will learn of what I have told you and use their influence to clear the names of all those brave sailormen who were miscalled and misunderstood before, during and in the years since RMS Titanic finally slipped below the surface of the North Atlantic ocean, taking so many with her.

"Sorry to prolong your 'pain', Captain; but before we wind-up here: there *is* one last - we think - important question we would like to ask you - it is a personal one."

OK! then... go ahead... I think my skin is thick enough.

"You have given us your opinion regarding the findings of the Official Inquiries regarding the conduct of certain individuals during and after the disaster and we note what you say. However' we wonder what your opinion is regarding what the world said and still believes about you and your conduct before and during that time?...You earlier quoted from the findings of the Official Inquiries; to help you answer this question, we now remind you what those same people wrote about you. First - the flowery Shakespearean oratory of Senator Smith in his report to the US Senate:

'Titanic though she was, his indifference to danger was one of the direct and contributing causes of this unnecessary tragedy, while his own willingness to die was the expiating evidence of his fitness to live. .....Those of us who knew him well - not in anger, but in sorrow - file one specific charge against him: Overconfidence and neglect to heed the oft-repeated warnings of his friends'

Then we have the brief, clinical verdict of the UK Inquiry which simply stated that excessive speed was to blame. In other words - you were going too fast."

Yes! I have read these bits of nonsense in great detail and conclude that they were, as I say - nonsense.

I can well imagine that clown - my namesake - Senator Smith - addressing the Forum at Rome way back in the olden days. In fact; these ancients had more ship- savvy than that man ever had. That gobble-de-gook translates much the same as the British version...I was going too fast despite warnings of clear and imminent danger.

As I have said before; those who have read the relevant evidence and more to the point - understood it and also read the evidence given by experienced Master Mariners at that time, will see very clearly that I never received any warnings of ice in my path and that all of the ice reported was to the north of my intended track.

In the real world of April 14, 1912, ship masters who

encountered ice kept up speed before they met it, then, if they could see it, stopped then went through it slowly or diverted around it without reducing speed. Only those like the 'Californian' which actually met with it, stopped for it. In fact: back in 1912...during the ice season...January to September...if every ship had slowed down for an ice report, it would have ended-up as a huge traffic-jamb in mid Atlantic

Incidentally; it wasn't a big ice berg that we hit - not like the giants shown in photographs claiming to be the culprit. In fact, it was barely the height of our boat deck which was 70 feet above the sea'

With these few words, I really must bid you all a final farewell. Once again - thank you all for listening to me. I hope this old face hasn't damaged you cameras.

No doubt; if my story ever gains public interest, you will let me know, but for now: Good-by and good luck to you and your families.

Milton Keynes UK
Ingram Content Group UK Ltd.
UKHW011008260624
444734UK00001B/17

9 798823 088367

USA Today bestselling author **Barb Han** lives in north Texas with her very own hero-worthy husband, three beautiful children, a spunky golden retriever/standard poodle mix and too many books in her to-read pile. In her downtime, she plays video games and spends much of her time on or around a basketball court. She loves interacting with readers and is grateful for their support. You can reach her at barbhan.com

Carla Cassidy is an award-winning, *New York Times* bestselling author who has written over 170 books, including 150 for Mills & Boon. She has won the Centennial Award from Romance Writers of America. Most recently she won the 2019 Write Touch Readers' Award for her Mills & Boon Heroes title *Desperate Strangers*. Carla believes the only thing better than curling up with a good book is sitting down at the computer with a good story to write.

Also by Barb Han

Marshals of Mesa Point
Ranch Ambush
Bounty Hunted

The Cowboys of Cider Creek
Rescued by the Rancher
Riding Shotgun
Trapped in Texas
Texas Scandal
Trouble in Texas
Murder in Texas

Also by Carla Cassidy

The Scarecrow Murders
Killer in the Heartland
Guarding a Forbidden Love
The Cowboy Next Door
Stalker in the Storm

Cowboys of Holiday Ranch
Cowboy Defender
Cowboy's Vow to Protect
The Cowboy's Targeted Bride
The Last Cowboy Standing

Discover more at millsandboon.co.uk